HELÉNE SMUTS

DITCH MEDIOCRITY

Learn how to take your team performance from average to incredible

*I dedicate this book to all the leaders
who are yet to read it but don't
think they need to…*

All rights reserved.
No part of this publication may be reproduced, stored in a retrieval system or transmitted in any form nor any means, electronically, mechanically, photocopying recording or otherwise without prior permission from the author and publisher.

DITCH MEDIOCRITY
Learn how to take your team performance from average to incredible
©2021 Heléne Smuts

Credo Growth, Claremont, South Africa

First print 2021
ISBN 978-0620-93824-2

Edited by Nazley Omar
Design and layout by Lindsay Peddie

Printed by Print on Demand
6 Koets Street
Parow Industria

contents

Contents

1. **Setting the stage** — 03
2. **The importance of social styles** — 12
3. **Understanding ego states** — 20
4. **Navigating tough conversations** — 30
5. **Your attitude as a leader** — 38
6. **Lead like a coach** — 46
7. **How to motivate your team** — 54
8. **Creating a safe work environment** — 60
9. **Building trust** — 66
10. **Effective listening skills** — 72
11. **Fostering a proactive team** — 78
12. **How to give amazing feedback** — 84

Acknowledgments — 91

Foreword

I never, ever imagined that I would write a book. I'm not an academic, I struggle with scientific research and I despise long, theoretical explanations of methodologies.

So you can be assured that this book has none of that. You will not read any scientific data or complex theories about leadership tools. Instead, this book will focus on:

→ What I've learnt about leadership and team development since I started developing people and high-performing teams in 2007.
→ Practical leadership tools, that I gained from many amazing leaders over the years.
→ How to implement these tools to take your team to high performance.

I first developed an online course called "Developing your own high performing team", which you can access with a QR code at the end of the book. The feedback from this course was incredible and several business leaders said they loved implementing the learnings. This led me to consider writing a book about the course. And just like that, an idea came to life. All I had to do was turn something I had already put out into the world into a different format – what could possibly go wrong, aside from experiencing a heightened sense of imposter syndrome…? *(Damn this feeling)*

For your own sake, if you want to learn about the scientific and data-driven facts about developing high performing teams, then you should turn to other books. There are a plethora and they are great. *(And I won't be offended)*

BUT: if you are keen to learn about team development and leadership tools that are practical, easy to understand and high impact, then read on.

What you can expect:
→ A quick explanation of various leadership and team development tools. At Credo Growth we use these tools for in-person and virtual workshops, so you can implement them whether you work face-to-face or virtually.
→ Examples and anecdotes of clients we have worked with.
→ A list of action steps to improve various aspects of your team's performance.
→ Visit our resources page: http://bit.ly/guidingaction

The idea is that as a leader, you take the learnings, implement them and start reaping the rewards of a high performing team. Hopefully this will turn you into someone that people love to follow and leave you feeling freaking great about the leader you have become.

I'm also going on the assumption that your business or the company that you work for already has its values, vision and key performance indicators in place.

Remember, information changes knowledge NOT behaviour, so don't assume that you can change things just by reading this book. YOU have to implement the learnings!

Mediocrity is just not an option!

> 💬 In this book, I have shared stories and learnings based on my experiences as a high-performance team facilitator. However, due to the nature of my work and the often sensitive conversations I have related to conflict and people, I have chosen not to mention my client's names, only the industries they work in. I respect the confidentiality I have with my clients and want to keep it that way.

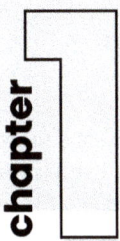

chapter 1

Setting the stage

When history books talk about revolutionary companies, they often focus on the success of an individual, but American business magnate Henry Ford would not have disrupted the motor industry without an efficient team on the assembly line, and Steve Jobs would not have achieved success without his business partner, Steve Wozniak.

"Great things in business are never done by one person. They are done by a team of people," Jobs famously said.

Regardless of how talented, driven or innovative a leader is, business is very much a team sport. The success of a sports team comes down to a group of individuals doing what's best for the greater good of the team. But how do iconic teams like Michael Jordan and the Chicago Bulls, or Lewis Hamilton and Mercedes Benz manage to come out on top time and time again? According to Bruce Tuckman, a renowned psychology professor, the key to success is an understanding of the team dynamic.

In 1965, Tuckman developed a model that describes the four stages that a team goes through before it can deliver optimal results. He explained that teams need to navigate the *forming* → *storming* → *norming* → *performing* stages in order to grow, tackle challenges and find solutions to achieve high performance. To help teams navigate these stages, leaders need to identify and understand which stage their team is at, before they can determine the action steps required to accelerate to the next stage.

Don't get me started on football teams.

Bruce Tuckman's team stages ────────────────

1
Forming

2
Storming

3
Norming

4
Performing

Forming

The forming stage of team development is all about settling in to a new role and getting acquainted with the team members. Like a first date or the honeymoon stage of a relationship, this is the period where people are keen to make a good impression and put their best foot forward. In a work environment, team members are at their best "LinkedIn behaviour" showing eagerness, politeness and excitement. Even though people appear super polite, they may experience inner turmoil or tension because they have a lot of questions about their new role, how they will fit into the team and what will be expected of them.

New teams aren't only formed as a result of the creation of a new company or department, it can happen any time new members or management come onboard. Business leaders often make the mistake of failing to prepare for new team members. I have seen many instances where an employee starts a new job but their desk is not ready or the rest of the team is unaware that a new person will be joining the team. This can significantly heighten the anxiety of the team members and set the team up for failure from the word go.

It's important that leaders don't ask people to start working immediately or expect teams to assimilate naturally. Instead, everyone should receive a proper orientation or introduction to build comfort and familiarity. Also implement steps to help team members glide through the forming phase and set them up for the phase to come.

How to lead a team in the forming stage

→ **Facilitate the introductions:** Set aside some time to introduce team members and highlight each person's role, skills and background. This way when problems surface, staff members will know who to get in touch with, which will help to streamline problem solving.

→ **Get to know your teammates:** People tend to be more cooperative and effective when they work with people they like. Help foster a relaxed work environment by doing some icebreaker activities or asking fun questions. When teammates bond over the latest Netflix series or their weekend plans, it lightens the mood and creates a sense of community.

→ **Establish goals and expectations:** The most important part of the forming stage is establishing clear roles, goals and direction. Team members need to understand exactly what is expected of them and how they fit into the bigger picture. If the team is working on a big project, break it into smaller, more achievable goals with a deadline for each one.

→ **Create a collaboration agreement:** Discuss how teammates will be expected to work together, how conflict will be resolved and how problems will be tackled. This relates to a psychological contract, which refers to the unspoken set of expectations that employees and organisations have of each other.

→ **Discuss the future:** Present these stages to the team and explain what is bound to happen in each. By understanding potential pitfalls, teammates will be better equipped to solve problems and transition more effectively through the different stages.

CHAPTER 1: *setting the stage*

2 Storming

Once the excitement of a new team or project starts to wear off, reality kicks in and the honeymoon comes to an end. This is the stage where everyone starts to feel the weight of the workload and people really get to know one another – flaws and all. Like a new couple, this is the stage where politeness falls away and you start to notice little grievances like leaving the toilet seat up or nagging too much.

This is also when the team starts to face challenges, whether it's a missed deadline, personality clashes or slow progress – discord is inevitable. Hierarchies and cliques start to form. There is often a lot of confusion and emotions can run high. During this phase, things seem to take longer and tasks are harder than anticipated. Remember that the tension between team members isn't always palpable, storming can brew <u>below the surface and can linger for years.</u> *This is NOT what you want!*

> We have a client in the tech space, where the team had moved past the storming phase. The team was doing well when a new person joined the team. Management failed to give her a proper induction so she didn't understand the company culture from the onset. For the first few weeks of the forming stage, everything seemed to be going well. Then her personality began to surface and she expressed discontent about how things were going. This caused a lot of tension between team members. The drama could have been avoided if the team leader had taken the time to properly navigate the forming phase and help the new teammate to settle in. Even if it's a small team, it's always necessary to give team members the time and space to assimilate to a change in a team. Don't neglect to implement the steps required in the forming stage to set the team up for success. If you don't work through them, you will inevitably have to deal with inter-team friction at a later stage.

Many businesses try to avoid or skip the negative aspects of the storming stage but it's crucial that a team goes through it. Just like in a healthy relationship where you discuss little annoyances and find a compromise, the same applies to a team setting. Learning to navigate conflict or challenges will make the team more effective in the long run. If leaders don't address the storming phase in the hopes that it will pass, the business may still perform and make a profit but it will result in unhappy team members.

CHAPTER 1: setting the stage

How to lead a team in the storming stage

→ **Address conflict:** During the storming stage, teammates are tempted to play the blame game or talk among themselves about problems. Conflict should not be feared. Help your team to develop the tools needed to address and resolve conflict as soon as tensions rise. Organise feedback sessions to give everyone time to express their concerns and encourage people to communicate and compromise. (We will talk more about giving and receiving feedback in later chapters.)

→ **Encourage leadership within the team.** Leadership shouldn't only be top down. Create a safe space for people to step up and take charge when they feel inspired or are capable. Mentorship and coaching are great ways to develop skills and competence. If you have one person that consistently causes trouble, it's a good idea to give them added responsibility. When a client of mine had issues with a troublemaker, the team leader decided to put them in charge of running daily meetings. After just two weeks, the troublemaker's entire attitude changed. The team was better aligned and there was more harmony, which allowed the team leader to get on with the strategic aspects of the business instead of micromanaging bickering teammates. *#winning*

→ **Focus on task performance:** Ensure that the focus is on task achievement and responsibility. The more people focus on the tasks at hand, the less time there is for arguing. Implement daily stand-up meetings, which is when attendees typically participate while standing. The discomfort of standing for long periods helps to keep the meetings short.

> If you'd like to find out more about implementing stand-up meetings or weekly huddles, check out the books *Scaling up* by Verne Harnish and *Traction* by Gino Wickman.

→ **Redefine goals and roles:** If team members are experiencing confusion or frustration, clarify what success looks like at each milestone. Discuss what is expected of each person.

Lesley Waterkant, founder and CEO of a South African brand experience agency called Colourworks, once said: "Identify people's lanes, stay out of people's lanes and own your own lane."

> To find out more about how to set up roles, take a look at the Function Accountability Chart and Process Accountability chart in *Scaling up* (p 46-57).

→ **Document solutions:** When you find a solution or process that is particularly effective, make a record of it so team members can refer to it when future problems arise.

→ **Revisit the collaboration agreement:** The collaboration agreement (*see Forming, page 4*) plays a critical role in the storming phase. Facilitate discussions about team member's behaviour, where things went wrong and what can be done to move forward.

→ **Don't be afraid to call a spade a spade:** There is no benefit to avoiding conflict. If it isn't addressed, it will fester. Show the team how to deal with conflict head on, yet respectfully. Plan what you are going to say and how you will address it. If you struggle, call a facilitator to assist with navigating the process. *Trust me!*

Dealing with conflict doesn't come naturally to everyone. Some employees may require training.

3. Norming

The norming stage is all about settling into a groove. In a relationship, once a couple has ironed out all the little irks and reached a compromise, they tend to get on famously. This is when a team becomes more supportive and cooperative. They learn to work together, genuine friendships start to form and they may even develop a few inside jokes.

The team may face challenges, but by this stage they have learnt how to communicate and compromise. People are able to move past conflict or disagreements and come up with solutions. They are also able to compensate in areas where fellow team members lack expertise and work together towards a common goal.

During the norming phase teams will experience an increase in productivity. While it's a comfortable place to be, the team is not yet at optimal performance. It's very easy to get stuck here. Even though things work well and there are no real complaints, the team's performance is mediocre.

Moving past norming to the performing phase doesn't mean you need to become the next listed business. This transition is just as important for small or medium-sized businesses because it allows you to have a much smoother operation. You have done all the work to get your team to this stage, so step up and develop your team further. If you're reading this as a leader, you have an obligation towards your team to develop them further. If you'd like to get an idea of what a meeting agenda looks like visit: http://bit.ly/guidingaction

How to lead a team in the norming stage

→ **Monitor progress:** Hold regular meetings to see if everyone is on track to reach their goals. When teammates take a step back to look at the larger picture it can lead to increased synergy and innovation.

→ **Ask team members to review their own progress:** Urge the team to ask themselves questions such as: What did I do well? What would I change if I had to do this again and why? This can be incredibly awkward in the beginning. One of my mentors warned me about how uncomfortable self-reflection meetings can be, but it's crucial that you push through. Tweak the daily stand-up meetings until they work for you but stick to the rules.

→ **Celebrate milestones:** It's important to acknowledge wins along the way as it keeps the team in good spirits. Recognise the efforts of the group, as well as individuals who work hard. Just because you don't feel inclined to celebrate small or big wins, it doesn't mean your team doesn't need it. Ask the team to come up with ways to celebrate wins and get them to implement it, but ensure that you take part.

→ **Tackle potential issues:** Identify your team's weaknesses and find ways to improve. Resolve potential problems by identifying solutions, action steps and any risks or assumptions. You do not need to do or own everything. Assign owners to take on responsibility, let go and trust a bit more. Then follow up on progress in your daily or weekly meetings.

→ **Give team members more control:** Allow members to assign their own tasks as this promotes team engagement. Provide learning opportunities for people to grow even further.

There is an example agenda at the end of the book for you to try. Tweak it until you find what works for your team.

4. Performing

For two people in a relationship, this is when you reach the much envied and desired #CoupleGoals status. When it comes to the workplace dynamic, this is when the catchphrase *Teamwork makes the dream work* becomes a reality! At this stage, team members are able to achieve optimal performance and are very self-sufficient. There is trust and synergy within the team.

The best part of this stage is the hunger for feedback. People want to continuously grow, so teammates are constantly asking for and giving feedback. No one takes offence because the culture is one of learning and doing better. Also, roles become more flexible and people feel comfortable enough to innovate or challenge the status quo without fear of rejection. When issues do arise, the team is able to work through it without affecting deadlines or productivity.

It's important to note that if a team faces challenges such as an increase in workload or a significant change in team dynamics, it may result in some team friction. If the team didn't have the time and space to navigate the storming stage, it may lead to discourse later because they don't have the know-how to navigate conflict. This is why it's important for teams to be given the tools to deal with pressure and conflict early on.

How to lead a team in the performing stage

→ **Cross functional learning:** This is a great time for people to gain a deeper understanding of where they fit into the value chain and what is expected of them. Then establish a culture of cross-functional learning and collaboration. It's important to offer teammates, even high achievers, the opportunity to upskill.

→ **Keep morale up:** If a project is particularly demanding or time consuming, team members may feel discouraged or weary towards the end. Keep spirits up through words of encouragement. Take note of where people are struggling. Is it their capabilities or their motivation? If a team member is struggling, address them individually and don't assume that one solution fits all.

A pizza party is always a good idea.

→ **Acknowledge and recognise efforts:** It's important to celebrate when a goal is reached or a project is completed. There are many ways to celebrate overcoming a massive challenge. Team members will work hard in the future if their current efforts are acknowledged and appreciated. I often see team leaders with strong driver type personalities forgetting to stop and acknowledge the shit show that the team just dealt with and this can cause resentment over time.

→ **Take time to reflect:** Before the team moves on to the next project, take an honest look at what went well and what didn't. Then discuss the action steps the team can implement moving forward. Think about:
- What worked well
- What didn't go well
- What could we have done differently?

Bruce Tuckman's team stages overview

4. Performing
Synergy & trust | Commitment
Feedback culture
New challenges | Highly flexible

- Encourage group decision-making & problem solving
- Cross-functional learning & knowledge share
- Celebrate!
- Keep comms & information flowing

1. Forming
Questioning | Show of eagerness
Politeness | Safe topics
Putting team structure together

- Provide clear expectations and instructions
- Have quick response times
- Create a collboration agreement
- Present the stages to discuss ways forward

3. Norming
Team is supportive | Lower anxiety
Clarity of roles | Setting priorities
Working with each other

- Recognise group & individual efforts
- Provide learning opportunities
- Encourage members to review their own progress
- Let team assign own tasks

2. Storming
High emotions | Conflict/cliques
Lack of participation | Blaming game
Uncomfortable/personalities surface

- Encourage leadership
- Create safe space for feedback & listening
- Increase task responsibilty
- Revisit collaboration agreement
- Facilitated team development process

Notes

5 Adjourning (a bonus stage)

There are times when work is completed or an organisation's needs change and team members go their separate ways. This stage wasn't part of Tuckman's original team model, it was added a decade later and it represents the end or dismantling of a team.

Team members will experience a range of feelings during the adjourning stage. Some may feel sad because it's the end of a chapter or anxious about the uncertainty of the future, while others may feel content with the team's achievements.

Every adjournment is different but it's important to do something to achieve a sense of closure. As the leader of a team, you will also experience a range of emotions. Regardless of your feelings, you need to acknowledge that teammates have built a connection with each other so parting ways may be difficult. Understand that people may need to mourn.

Who's coming with me?

When a team member leaves, it's important for the team to consider the following:
- What good came from having this member on board?
- What did we learn from the experience?
- What type of person do we want to employ moving forward?

How to lead a team in the adjourning stage

→ **Tie up loose ends:** Complete any outstanding work and notify relevant stakeholders of the team's dissolution.

→ **Formalise the end of the team:** Acknowledge the contributions of both the team and individuals.

→ **Check out:** The circumstances of adjourning will dictate the type of closure you strive for. It can be valuable to have a farewell or ceremony where people can discuss the good, the bad and the laughs. It's also important to discuss the lessons learnt.

→ **The exit interview:** Don't do this simply to tick a box. It's important to really listen to what people have to say, particularly if they aren't leaving on good terms. There is valuable information in exit interviews and if you listen without defending or justifying yourself, you will learn a great deal about your team and where you can make performance changes.

And the times they wanted to kill each other!

> *A former client in the above-the-line marketing industry had a really high staff turnover. When I went to investigate and started speaking to people who were leaving the company, I found that many employees decided to leave because of the business founder's personality. While he ran an incredibly successful company, he had trouble retaining his A-players. The reason was his approach to his team. He failed to show his appreciation to his staff and he often made jokes at their expense, calling them "half-day workers" if they left at 17:30. When he asked me to find a solution to the problem, however, he told me to look at the team but not at him.*
>
> *As leaders, this is something all of us need to keep in mind. We can't expect people to come in and "fix" our team, if we are not willing to be part of the process and be open to understanding that we might be part of the problem. The company is no longer a client due to the founder's expectations and his unwillingness to look at his own development.* :)

If you are a leader, you need to be open to learning and growing. **People will not stick around to propel your business to high performance if you aren't willing to address your own flaws.** And that's what this book is about: to help you to become a leader that everyone wants to follow.

Chapter checklist

- [ ] Explain the different phases to your team.
  Then together, as a team, do the following:
- [ ] Analyse which phase the team is currently at .
- [ ] Identify what is keeping the team in this phase.
- [ ] Discuss and agree on action steps to move the team forward.
- [ ] Assign different tasks to 'owners' to allow for accountability.
- [ ] Report back on progress in daily or weekly meetings.
- [ ] Read more about effective meetings in *Scaling up* by Verne Harnish and *Traction* by Gino Wickman.

chapter 2

The importance of social styles

'm sure you have heard the saying "treat people how you want to be treated". I think in leadership this phrase should rather say: "treat and engage with others how they want to be treated". Being a leader requires you to understand what really drives and inspires individuals.

Some team members prefer direct, to-the-point communication, while others respond better to a warm, nurturing approach. What works for one teammate may not work for the other, so interacting with everyone the same way can be counterproductive. It's important to be true to yourself but grow a pair and try to understand who your team members are. Don't expect everyone to be like you.

I am not saying you should change who you are or be inauthentic, but you can certainly take some time to really understand your team members and make a damn effort to communicate and engage in tasks in a way that they understand.

At Insight Discovery, we focus on adapting and connecting. If you really want to understand someone, you need to adapt your style so that it works for both of you. This is critical to having great working relationships and achieving high performance.

Each person has a unique social style, which refers to the natural way they interact, communicate and resolve conflict with others.

Developed by psychologists David Merrill and Roger Reid in the 1950s, the Social Style Model outlines four distinct social styles: **Driver, Analytic, Amiable** and **Expressive**. These social styles are so insightful that characters in films and series are often modeled after them. The four friends in the HBO series *Sex and the City,* and the main characters in the movie *The Hangover,* each embody one of the social styles.

Let me be clear, I'm not saying that there are only four styles. I use this model in this book and in the online leadership course as it is easy to understand and quick to implement. There are many amazing tools out there. At Credo Growth, we make extensive use of Enneagram and Insights Discovery that have up to 72 different personality styles, with even more variants within each type. It's not about putting people into boxes, it's about understanding how people interact and learning how to tap into the different styles available to us.

The Social Style Model assesses individuals based on two traits:
Assertiveness refers to the way a person presents their point of view. An "ask assertive" person takes time to make decisions because they ask more questions and are more process oriented. Whereas, a "tell assertive" person makes decisions quickly. They prefer to make statements as opposed to asking questions and they are more results oriented.
Responsiveness analyses how individuals display their emotions. People who demonstrate controlled responses are low on the responsiveness scale and tend to be more rigid. While those with emotional responses are more expressive with their words and body language.

Based on the descriptions above, you can determine which of the four social styles is your primary and secondary style of communicating. The styles below are the four main social styles.

Driver

People with this social style are independent, decisive and efficient. They are high on the assertive scale and they usually keep their emotions under control. They operate well under pressure and they work hard to achieve results. Drivers are valuable in a team because they help to steer a team forward. In business, Drivers excel in positions such as Managing Director or Chief Executive Officer where decisions need to be made. Well known people who often lead with a Driver style are Henry Ford and Mark Zuckerberg.

The downside of the Driver social style is that they can be insensitive, inflexible, autocratic and demanding. They tend to put a lot of pressure on the team because they expect results quickly. Drivers need to work on listening to others and practicing empathy and patience.

I'm a Driver and it took me very long to step into the power of my social style. *Because I used to feel so damn guilty about it.* It's easy to only see the negative side of the Driver style, and if you do, you risk losing out on the incredible energy that a driver can bring.

I have worked with many teams where the Driver style was not present or very low, and they all experienced the same issues: slow or stagnant progress and a lack of accountability. Not having a Driver to steer the team or having one that feels stifled due to the judgment from the other styles could negatively affect the team's productivity.

Tips for tapping into your inner Driver
→ **Focus on results.** It's natural for Drivers to focus on goals and deadlines so harness your energy to deliver on your promises.
→ **Take charge when necessary.** When faced with a tough situation or scenario, team members might be hesitant to step up. This is a great opportunity to show your leadership skills.
→ **Make swift decisions.** Drivers are very good at being decisive so practice making timely choices.

CHAPTER 2: *the importance of social styles*

> **How to communicate with a Driver**
>
> *Ensure that all communication is clear, straightforward and concise. Don't bore them with irrelevant details, rather focus on goals and the actions that are required to succeed. Don't make ambiguous remarks or say anything that you aren't able to back up. Speak with confidence and avoid appearing anxious or flustered.*

2. Analyser

Individuals with this social style tend to be serious, organised and calculating. They are "ask assertive", which means they ask a lot of questions and they don't show their emotions often. Their main goal is getting things right so they are very thorough and logical. Analysers are an asset to a team because they work conscientiously to ensure quality and accuracy, bringing with them a sense of calm and structure. They are well suited to positions such as Finance Director or Chief Operating Officer. Famous faces who often tap into the Analyser style include Albert Einstein and Angela Merkel.

The negative aspects of this social style include being inflexible and critical, as well as cold and distant. They are often slow to make decisions because they gather information and painstakingly consider all the options, which can sometimes lead to analysis paralysis. Analysers should work on being more approachable, sharing ideas and learning to collaborate.

I've worked with teams where there wasn't an Analyser on board and this is when things tend to slip through the cracks and mistakes are made. For example, there was a digital marketing agency where the person checking the editing did not tap into their analytical style and content was posted online with spelling mistakes. This is bad for branding and bad for profit!

I also have a fintech client, where we decided to bring in an analytical CEO because the founders of the business were a bunch of creative cowboys. Once the CEO started implementing structure and putting procedures in place, the team began operating effectively. This is because he was able to provide the team with structure and this greatly affected the productivity. *which is what they call themselves*

It's important, however, to ensure that you don't lose the entrepreneurial flair of the business, which can sometimes be stifled by Analysers. Therefore, it's important to focus on areas of development, spearhead loads of feedback loops and challenge the Analyser when there are rules that can be broken.

Tips for tapping into your analytical side
→ **Focus on the details.** Analysers pick up on small details that other team members miss. Take your time to ensure that your work is accurate and focus on detailed tasks.
→ **Gather information.** There are certain times, such as when you are choosing a supplier or buying equipment, when you need to do proper research. Analysers are good at gathering data and making an informed decision. Take note of your team member's engagement and motivation.

How to communicate with an Analyser

Always be prepared. Provide an Analyser with detailed, accurate information and if you are doing a presentation, give supporting data and research. Don't assume that silence indicates disinterest or push them to make decisions because they need time to think things through and reflect. Don't appear to be disorganised or frivolous and avoid using exaggerations.

Just get to the point.

3. Amiable

Often referred to as team players, Amiables tend to be easy-going, loyal and supportive. They are "ask assertive", which means they tend to ask questions rather than make statements and they are quick to express their emotions. Building and maintaining relationships are very important to people with amiable personalities. They are good listeners, excel at cooperating with others and they need to feel appreciated by the people around them. In a corporate setting, they are well suited to the position of a trainer, Client Relationship Director or Human Resource Manager. Celebrities with Amiable leading styles include Jennifer Aniston, Princess Diana and Warren Buffet.

The negative characteristics of Amiables include being timid, unassertive or stubborn. They try to please everyone so they can be indecisive and too compliant. When they feel undervalued their self-esteem takes a knock and they can become anxious. It's important for Amiables to work on their assertiveness and focus less on what others think.

In the past, I developed an unhealthy business relationship with an Amiable. They would agree to do certain tasks in meetings and later when I followed up, they would say that they want to revisit the task or required more time, usually when the deadline had already passed.

What I learnt from this experience is that you need to create a safe space for people in meetings where they can admit that they need more time or give them time to digest information and make decisions. Not addressing issues in meetings, with the aim of avoiding conflict will only lead to "storming" environments.

CHAPTER 2: *the importance of social styles*

When you lead a team of people, you have a responsibility to tap into your Amiable style. This doesn't mean your submissive, timid side. It refers to the part of you that really puts time aside and listens, without thinking about tasks or productivity but your team and their needs. If you know that you struggle with this, make sure that you have someone (such as a second-in-charge) within the team that can fulfill that role. No team can flourish with only Drivers and Analysers.

> **Tips for tapping into your inner Amiable**
> → **Provide support.** Take the time to make people feel comfortable and create a sense of harmony. Strive to become a team player.
> → **Learn to listen.** There is great value in building solid professional relationships. Ensure that you actually listen to your teammates and guide them if necessary.

How to communicate with an Amiable: Amiables need to feel respected and secure in their relationships. Therefore, it's best to avoid being overbearing or too direct when speaking to them. Instead, communicate in a friendly manner and take the time to build rapport. Ask their opinion and make them feel valued. Give them time to process information and do not pressure them to make decisions.

4. Expressive

The most extroverted of the personality types, Expressives are open, eager to engage and creative. They are "tell assertive" so they have a lot to say and they often express their emotions. They are fun to be around because they are high-energy and they have a natural way of motivating people. Expressive people add value to a team because they are innovative and intuitive. They make great creatives, Marketing Managers and Designers. Examples of people with Expressive leadership styles are Jim Carey, Madonna, Steve Jobs and Oprah Winfrey.

Popularity and recognition are important to Expressives, so they can be seen as attention seeking or drama queens. They have a short attention span and often times have unrealistic expectations. They are incredibly passionate so they get frustrated when people are not excited about their ideas. It's important for Expressives to learn how to follow through with ideas and pay attention to detail.

Express yourself
You've got to make him
Express himself
Hey, hey, hey, hey
– Madonna

Expressives are often seen as ditsy or not credible which is a very big misconception. However, if your team is made up of solely Expressives, you may have an issue with follow through and focus.

> One of our clients has a strong expressive co-founder, who tends to focus on technical and software development, but he neglects the strategic side of the business. Credo Growth was bought in because the co-founder started to drop the ball by falling behind on client projects.
>
> Through a series of team development workshops and personality profiling sessions, what became very apparent is that his exclusion from strategic meetings over a period of time slowly took away his high energy and negatively impacted his motivation. He became bogged down with the details and his motivation levels dropped. While this may seem obvious to others, it isn't always to the person experiencing it. When you are struggling, it requires deep conversations and reflection to figure out why there is a drop in productivity.

It's very important that you don't try to put an Expressive in a box. **Yes, give them boundaries** but allow them to play freely within those boundaries.

Tips for tapping into your expressive style:

→ **Get creative.** Even the most analytical people have a creative side. It's important for everyone to be imaginative and take the time to think outside the box.

→ **Generate enthusiasm.** Expressives are very good at creating hype and excitement around their ideas. Passion goes a long way, in any business. Sometimes people just need to be assured that they have permission to think outside of the box.

How to communicate with an Expressive

Expressives work best when they have the time and space to innovate and be spontaneous. Avoid discussing details or theories at length as this will bore or frustrate them. They fear rejection so consider their ideas before you simply dismiss them. Embrace their warmth and talkativeness and show some excitement about the things they are passionate about.

CHAPTER 2: *the importance of social styles*

None of the social styles are better than the others. In fact, a workplace functions best when there is a mixture of all four, because each one brings something different to the table. It's crucial for leaders to understand what their social style is, as well as how to capitalise on their strengths and improve on their weaknesses.

Each one of us possesses elements of all four styles, but it's the intensity of each style that differs. For example, my Analyser isn't strong. It's my third style, however, I have worked on developing it and now I'm quite good at spending time on financials or deep diving into research. I'm able to do it for short bursts of time before my energy is drained. Think about what energises you and what leaves you exhausted. Take note of your own style and how it affects the way you lead on good and bad days.

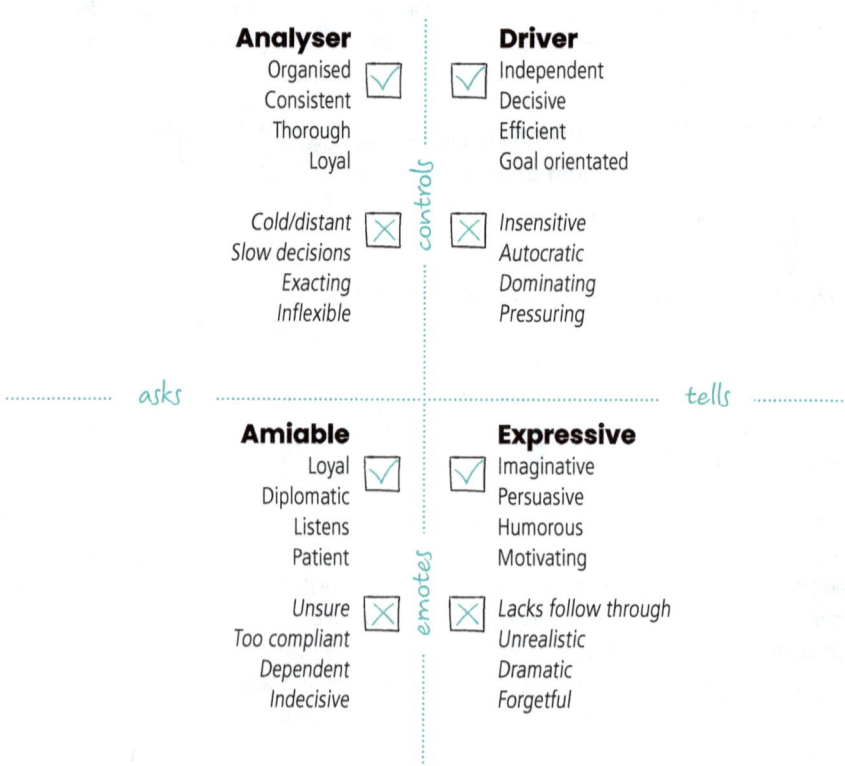

DAVID MERRILL AND ROGER REID'S SOCIAL STYLE MODEL

It's also beneficial to contemplate which social style your teammates are. When you communicate with someone consider how you can match their body language and word choice to make them feel more comfortable or responsive. You don't need to abandon your natural communication style but connecting with someone in their style and in a way that makes them feel comfortable will make them more inclined to respond positively.

Also take the time to encourage team members to consider what their styles are. Ask them what their specific style adds to the team. What are their shortfalls and what is holding them back? When people are able to understand why their teammates think and act the way they do, it can improve the harmony and effectiveness of the entire team.

> *One of our clients, a big data analyst company, struggled with engagement among team members. This became a problem because a team of Analysers just don't communicate as well as Amiables or Expressives do. To address the issue, we arranged profile dates, where everyone had the opportunity to go on a one-on-one coffee or beer date. Before the date, each person had to read the other person's profile and then together they discussed what they found interesting about each other and what they would like to see more of from the other person. We have implemented this with many of our clients to ensure that team members are being heard and are able to be their true selves.*

Chapter checklist

- [ ] Gain a better understanding of your own personality. Crystal Knows *(www.crystalknows.com)* offers free tests that offer great insights into the different styles. If you are after a more in-depth, detailed analysis like the ones we use when working with clients, Insight Discovery or Enneagram are the way to go.
- [ ] Do a team workshop where each member identifies how their strengths and weaknesses affect the team.
- [ ] Start using social style language in your team.
- [ ] Set up engagement sessions where team members can share and learn more about each other's styles and their preferred ways of communication.

Understanding ego states

Have you ever had a conversation that left you feeling small? Or do you find yourself being very critical of certain individuals? Or maybe you've witnessed an adult tantrum. All of these behaviours can be explained through a simple model of communication, called **ego states.**

Psychiatrist Eric Berne developed this psychological theory and it is one of my favourite theories to use when analysing communication and conflict in the workplace because it helps you to understand your own behaviour, as well as why people respond to you in the way that they do.

The ego state model is part of the theory of Transactional Analysis and it's made up of three ego states: **Parent, Adult** and **Child.** They do not necessarily focus on your ego but more on your behaviour. Each person embodies all three of these states and we shift between them. The ego state a person activates at any given time depends on the situation. It is influenced by the relationship they have with the person they are talking to, how they are feeling at the time, and how the other person is treating them. Please don't think of it as if you are a child or a parent to someone, these ego states refer to the behaviour that is demonstrated.

To explain the ego states, I'm going to use a very basic example to demonstrate how the inner voices in our head works.

It's the company's townhall meeting today, you wake up and have the following conversation with yourself.

Then your train of thought changes.
→ Man, it's such an amazing day to go surfing. The waves are perfect so I'm going to skip the meeting because no one will miss me and boy will I have fun.
→ What if someone sees me? I would feel so guilty and the embarrassment about not showing up as a leader would stay with me for a while. I really don't want to disappoint the CEO…
→ BUT, I've worked so hard, I really deserve a break and this is the perfect time to be kind to myself…
→ Yes, but I'm so far behind as a leader. I better pull up my socks as everyone else is doing a better job than me at the moment. I'm behind on my targets and going surfing

would just show people how useless I actually am...
→ Hold on, all the other leaders in this business milk their sick leave, it's about time I pull a sickie! Screw it and screw everyone else, it's my turn to take a "sick day".
→ Actually now that I'm thinking about it... I've worked hard and I deserve a break, but I'm behind on my targets and it's so important that I show up and set an example. So I think it would be better to plan ahead and take some time off when the team doesn't need me. This way I can show up for my team and take care of my own wellbeing.

Now consider these inner voices as you read about the different ego states. Can you identify which thoughts correspond to each of the ego states?

CHILD EGO STATE

This state is characterised by all the impulses that come naturally to an infant, and it manifests itself through the thoughts, feelings and behaviours you learnt during your childhood.

It's based on the experiences that a newborn baby has from the time they are born up until the age of six months. This is when you experience bodily sensations like hunger and tiredness, you act accordingly and then people react to you. What often happens is that as you grow older, you sometimes take on your parent's ego states or their "stuff". *Just think about how kids react to situations.*

Responses in this state are primarily driven by emotions and experiences. There are three kinds of child ego states.

→ **Free Child:** People in this state are often spontaneous, curious, creative, genuine and a lot of fun. It's the part of a person that loves feeling free and experiencing pleasure. They often say phrases like "wow" or "I'm in". However, a free child can also be selfish, impulsive, inconsiderate and naïve because they are so focused on doing what they want. They also have poor self-awareness.

→ **Adaptive Child:** Positive characteristics of this state include being polite, adaptable, flexible and considerate. Common phrases include "please" and "thank you". They are good at taking ownership and apologising when they make a mistake. However, this is a problematic state because this is when individuals try to change and adapt their feelings and behaviour in response to the people around them. They tend to make themselves small in the presence of others and they are submissive. They may pass up opportunities because they fear that someone else can do it better. This is when learned feelings such as guilt, fear, depression and anxiety creep in. An Adaptive Child constantly says "sorry" because they are responsible but lack confidence.

CHAPTER 3: *understanding ego states*

→ **Rebellious Child:** When a person enters this state, they are assertive, they have the ability to say "no" and they stand their ground. They do, however, behave in a way that is typical of an insubordinate child. They say phrases such as "forget it" or "whatever" and slam doors or storm off. They rebel against any kind of authority and they can be rude, destructive and uncooperative.

ADULT EGO STATE

This is the most reasonable, grown-up state where people don't base their decisions on emotion but on rational, truth and experience. This state is based on our experiences from the age of six months to about three years. My transactional analysis trainer always says: "The Adult is the little professor." This is when you begin learning strategies for problem solving. It's the time when you figure out how to best survive in the environment you are in.

When people are in the Adult state, they focus on the here and now and adopt a factual, objective point of view. They also take the time to question reality, think things through and look for the best outcome. They ask a lot of questions because they are concerned with the how, what, who, when and why. They are very observant. They don't react aggressively or try to control other people.

The downside of this ego state, however, is that if you are constantly in it, it can be boring because there may be a lack of passion, excitement and innovation.

PARENT EGO STATE

The Parent state is based on our experiences from the age three until 12. This is when we learn to navigate the rules that the "bigger people" have set for us. *Such as your parents, siblings or teachers.*

The way you behave in this state is influenced by the values, feelings and behaviours that you learnt from your parents and other authoritative figures. The Parent ego state comprises of two types:

→ **Critical Parent:** People in this ego state are good at being fair, setting boundaries and implementing structure or discipline. Common phrases include "you should", "you ought to" or "you must". They may speak with their hands on their hips and do a lot of finger pointing. They can be critical of anyone who doesn't meet their expectations and they can be condescending. In this state, individuals can be controlling, inflexible, dominant and judgmental.

→ **Nurturing Parent:** As the name suggests, this ego state is encouraging, comforting, empathetic and supportive. Nurturing Parents offer people in a Child ego state a place of safety and comfort, which is conducive for their growth and development. Common phrases include "well done", "good job" or "let me do it for you". The downside is that when you operate from Nurturing Parent you can be overprotective, smothering and disempowering. Remember that if you keep saving your team members, you are taking away their ability to learn and gain independence.

It's important to remember that each of us has all of these ego states submerged within us. For example, when I'm in the workplace and pressed for time, my Critical Parent kicks in and I can come across as really demanding and judgmental. However, when I'm with my older brothers and sisters, I become an Adaptive Child.

No one stays in one ego state. It's common for a person to transition to different ego states depending on how someone treats them. For instance, I could be in a good adult space but when someone addresses me in a condescending way, it invites me into a Child ego state in that moment. The key is to understand that ego states are situation and context specific. When you are drawn into a certain state, consider how you react to it and why you react so quickly.

What's also important to mention is that each ego state has pros and cons. The ideal way to communicate is to identify which ego state would be best to deliver a message. Then ensure that you tap into the positive aspects of each ego state, which we refer to as the "okay, okay" box, which means that both the sender and the receiver of the message leave the interaction feeling okay. By harnessing the constructive qualities of each ego state, you can deliver a bulls-eye message every time.

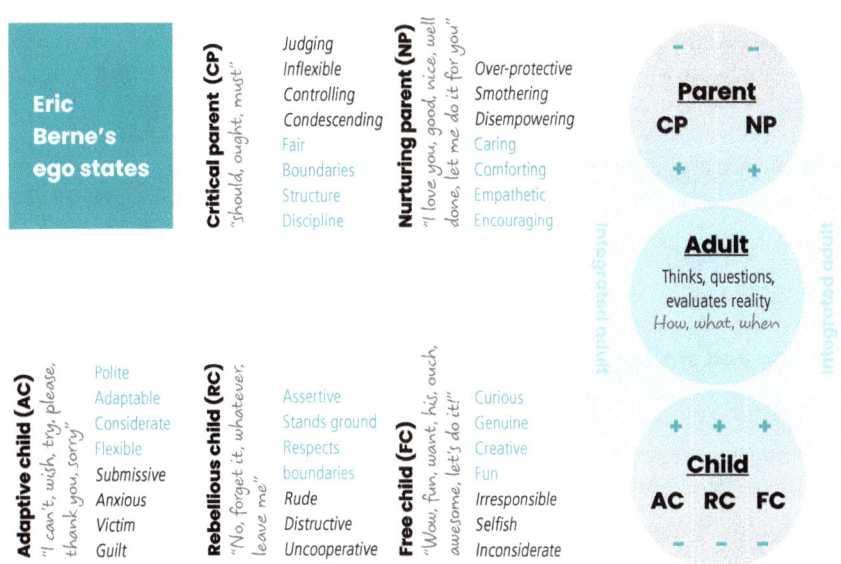

CHAPTER 3: *understanding ego states*

Which ego state are you mostly in?

Once you understand the three ego states and how they manifest, consider which state you occupy the most. Then determine how you can improve your communication through the following steps:

> → **Complete your ego-gram** *(use the template on the right):* The first step is to draw your own ego-gram based on how you currently see yourself as a leader. Do some honest reflection and determine how much time you spend in each of these states, as well as which situations lead you to behave in a negative way. For example, my Critical Parent is quite high, while my Nurturing Parent is low. My Adult ego state is high. My Rebellious Child is on the high side, my Adaptive Child is low and my Free Child is relatively high.
>
> *[margin note: This was learnt. It wasn't naturally high.]*
>
> What effect does this have on your team? Consider how this impacts the team's engagement, motivation and performance. Contemplate which ego state you channel with teammates, in meetings and in your personal relationships. For example, because my Nurturing Parent is so low, I may not notice when a team member needs some support, which is something that I need to work on.
>
> → **Design your ideal ego-gram:** Think about what your ego-gram would look like in an ideal world. How can you harness the positive aspects of your ego states and minimise the downsides? The aim shouldn't be for all the ego states to be on the same level, but for you to determine what is most effective in different roles. For example, I could work on lowering my Critical Parent and improving my Adaptive Child so instead of judging, I need to listen better especially when team members make suggestions or put forward ideas.
>
> → **Identify action steps:** Formulate a list of steps you can follow to bridge the gaps. Saying that you need to be more caring or more assertive is too vague. You need to be specific. For example, to lower my Rebellious Child I could commit to thinking things through and not immediately saying "no" when a team member makes a suggestion. If you want to reduce your Adaptive Child, you could make a commitment to voice your opinion or ideas at least once in each meeting. To boost your Nurturing Parent, take the time to have a casual chat with a team member once a week and make sure you really show interest in them.
>
> → **Get your team involved:** Explain the different ego states to your teammates and get them to draw up their own ego-gram. As a team, discuss when negative interactions tend to take place. Ask everyone to analyse which ego states come to the fore, why it happens and how it can be addressed. Encourage team members to share their insights such as "what we need is for you to dial up your Free Child" or "please watch your Critical Parent in meetings".

How do ego states affect a team?

Now that you know how ego states manifests themselves in individuals, I'd like to look at how it plays out when two people are involved. Whenever one person says something and the other person responds, a transaction takes place. It's important to remember that when two people come together, each one comes with their own set of six ego states, which is why communication is so complex. According to Berne, there are three types of transactions. There are three examples below to give you an idea of how ego states can manifest.

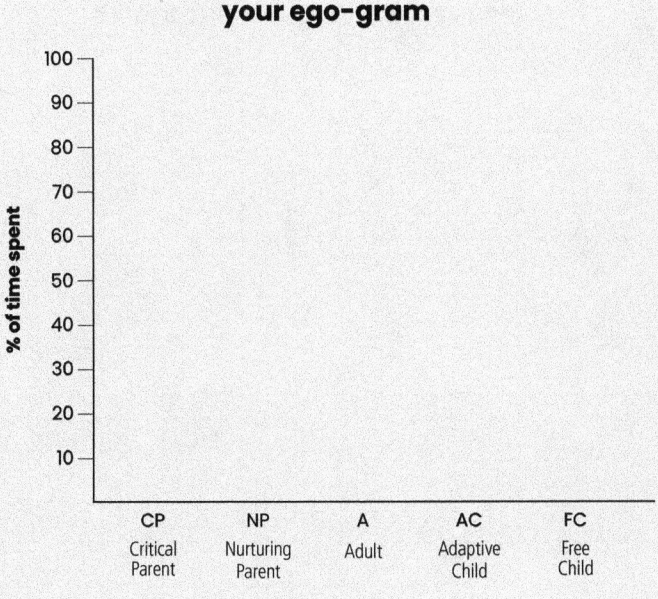
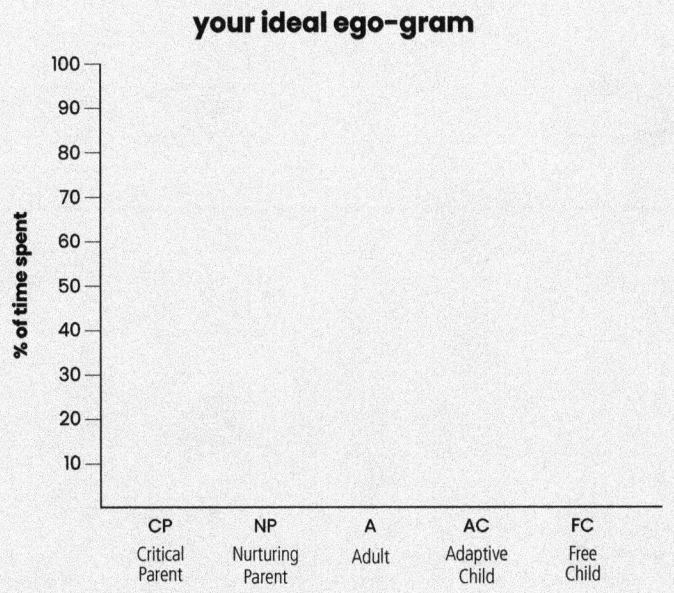

CHAPTER 3: *understanding ego states*

Guess your colleagues' ego states

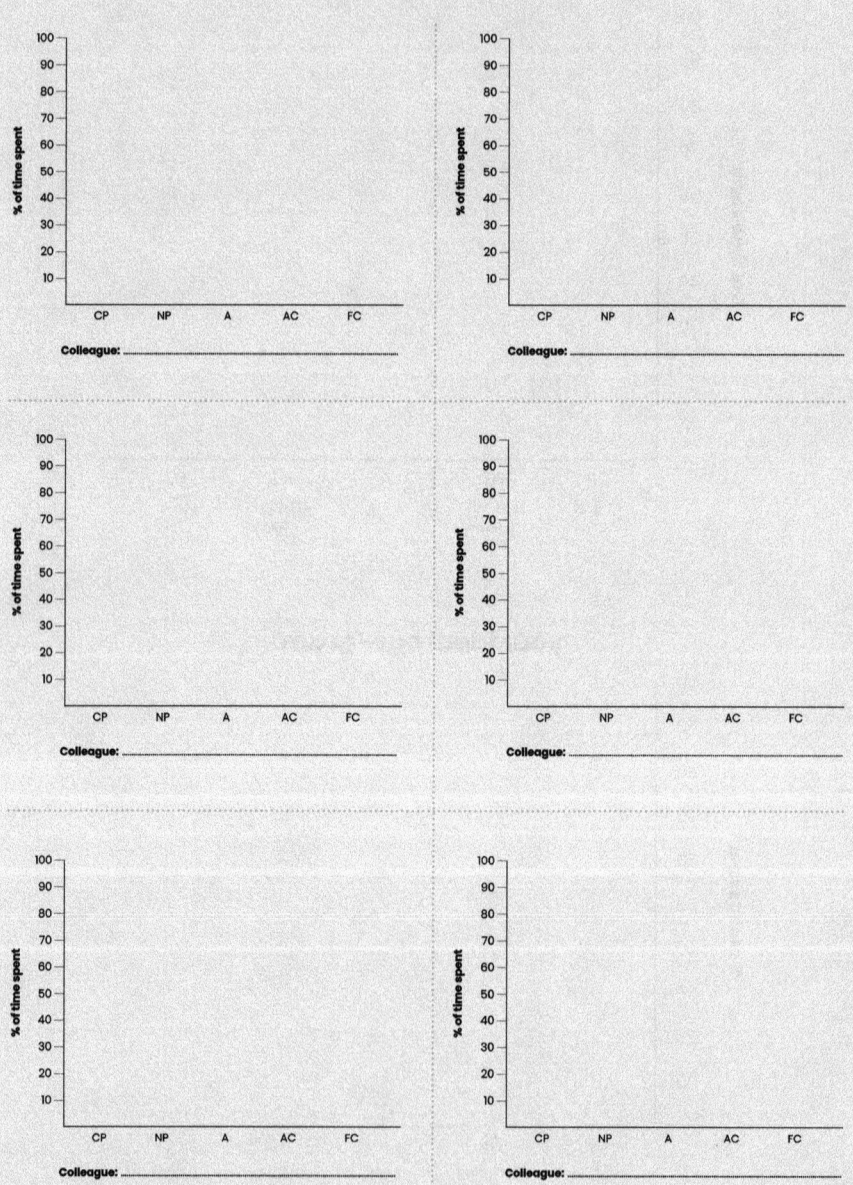

1 **Complimentary/parallel transactions:**
Communication works well when the activated ego states are complimentary or in harmony with each other. This occurs when a person invites someone to engage and the person responds in a manner that the other person expects. This way, there are no misunderstandings or conflict. Examples of complimentary transactions include:

→ **Adult to Adult:** According to Berne, this is the most effective and fruitful interaction in the workplace because both people are speaking respectfully and looking for the best result. For example, two colleagues discussing a failed project.
Person A: "Let's discuss what went wrong."
Person B: "Yes, I'm keen to see how we can improve."

→ **Parent to Parent:** This kind of interaction takes place when both people come from a place of experience and they are both either critical or nurturing in that moment. For example, two colleagues complaining about a workplace grievance.
Person A: "The delivery is delayed. It's so frustrating."
Person B: "I know. I'm fed up with our suppliers."

→ **Child to Child:** An interaction between two people in Child ego states would differ depending on whether it is the Free, Rebellious or Adaptive state. In the Free ego state, people would tap into their playful and spontaneous side. For example, two colleagues discussing ditching work.
Person A: "It's Friday, I'm not in the mood to work."
Person B: "I agree. Shall we go for a long lunch?"

→ **Parent to Child:** This can be a complimentary interaction as long as the both parties respond in the way that the other anticipated. For example, if a manager sees a team member arrive late but the interaction does not escalate. *complimentary doesn't necessarily mean healthy*
Person A: "Why are you late?"
Person B: "The traffic was terrible. I'm sorry."
Person A: "Okay."

2 **Crossed transactions**
This kind of transaction occurs when there is a breakdown in communication, which happens when the receiver forms the wrong impression about the sender's message, or the receiver responds in a different ego state than the sender anticipated. This often results in conflict or uneasiness for one or both parties.

CHAPTER 3: *understanding ego states*

→ **Parent to Child:** This happens when one person addresses the other in a Parent state expecting an Adapting Child response, but they get a Rebellious Child instead. For example, a manager asks about the progress of a task.
Person A: "When will you submit your proposal?"
Person B: "Why are you always nagging me?"

→ **Child to Parent:** A transaction of this nature occurs when a person approaches someone from a Child state, expecting a Nurturing Parent response, but they get a Critical Parent response instead.
Person A: "I'm so sorry I missed my deadline."
Person B: "You are so incompetent."

3 Hidden transactions

It's important to remember that when we communicate it's not only about what we say, but how we say it. A lot of meaning is conveyed through tone, facial expressions and body language. Think about sarcasm or dry humour, where the message is all in the delivery.

This kind of transaction can occur when someone is being passive aggressive. For example, when a team member arrives late to work and a colleague says:

 *Yip, you've been busted.*

Person A (as B walks in): "I wonder what the time is?"
Person B: "I know I'm late, no need to make a big deal out of it."
Person A: "I didn't say anything, I was just wondering what the time is."

Hidden transactions can also take place when there is a discrepancy between what we say and what we mean. For example, if two colleagues are being flirtatious.
Person A: "So are we working late today?" *(with an allusive smile)*
Person B: "Oh no, not again." *(with a wink)*

How to make ego states work for you

If there is one thing I want you to take from this book, it is that we send people invitations to communicate with us. So often we blame others for the way they communicate with us, but we need to consider how we address them. As a leader, if you approach someone in Critical Parent, you need to be prepared for a range of responses.

For example, if you say to a team member: "I cannot believe this is wrong. I'm getting tired of telling you this."

What you are hoping is that the person responds in Adaptive Child and says something like: "I'm so sorry. It won't happen again."

But there is a chance that they could respond in Rebellious Child instead and say: "Well if you're so tired of explaining it to me, why don't you just do it yourself?"

This could prompt you to go even further into your Critical Parent ego state and the team member to go into heightened Rebellious Child, which will result in conflict. This is why communication is so complex and it can spiral so quickly into a disagreement.

As a leader you need to be careful of how you construct and deliver your messages. If you speak in Critical Parent, you are inviting a response from a Child ego state and you just don't know which one you will get.

Conflict could also arise if you don't respond the way someone expects you to. For example, if a team member says to you: "I'm so sorry I missed my deadline. Is it possible for you to help me?" They are inviting you to respond in Nurturing Parent and are expecting you to say something along the lines of: "That's okay. I know you've been stressed. What can I do to help?"

If you are having a bad day, it could be very tempting to jump straight into Critical Parent and berate them but how will this help the situation? The best response would be to change to integrated Adult ego state and tap into the other ego states to support your statement or conversation. This would invite them to move into Adult too.

The most suitable response would be: "I noticed that you missed your deadline. What is your plan to get it done? Think about why this happened so it doesn't happen again."

You are showing the person that you respect them but you are tackling the issue. The Adult focuses on the factual, logical side of things. As a leader, you need to take note of what it looks like when you communicate in your Parent or Child ego states. Work on addressing people in Adult and inviting them to do the same so that interactions are respectful and effective while also utilising the positive aspects of the other ego states.

It's beneficial for a team to get together to discuss ego states and conflict. Get teammates to unpack particular situations that resulted in conflict. Ask them to consider how it started, which ego states were at play and where the transaction went wrong. Then discuss how to prevent similar situations in the future.

Chapter checklist

- [ ] Understand the positives and negatives of each ego state.
- [ ] Unpack the different types of transactions and how we send invitations to which people respond.
- [ ] Ask your team where they've seen these types of transactions in the team. Ask them for actual examples and debrief them together.
- [ ] Communicate more effectively using the knowledge of the ego-states.

Chapter 4

Navigating tough conversations

Difficult conversations are an inevitable part of leadership. Many leaders struggle to find the right words, whether it's informing a client about a setback, addressing a team member's body odour, or speaking to a colleague about the fact that they are not living up to the values of the business.

awkward :(

It's essential to prepare for a difficult conversation before you undertake it. Shooting from the hip could result in one or both parties responding in a reactive manner, which could lead to a breakdown in the relationship.

> One of our clients in the innovations space had a Director who was an integral part of the software development design team due to his technical knowledge. The issue was that this Director missed deadlines, failed to communicate about projects and neglected certain technical aspects of the business. This created a massive upset in the business and team members started to resign because they felt responsible for the inefficiency and that their efforts were leading them nowhere. It went so sour that they needed external intervention.
>
> So we held a crucial conversations workshop with the team and the Director in question. To facilitate the process, we followed the steps outlined in the pages that follow to make sure the conversation was as smooth and productive as possible.

The following steps are from the book *Crucial Conversations: Tools for Talking When Stakes Are High* by Al Switzler, Joseph Grenny, and Ron McMillan. **Remember that in order to implement these steps, you don't necessarily need a workshop. You can tackle difficult conversations anywhere, at any time.**

This book is amazing!

1 Start with the heart

Before you dive into a difficult conversation do some introspection and consider the following:

→ What would you like the outcome of the conversation to be?
→ What don't you want to happen during the conversation?
→ What kind of relationship do you want with the person?

By envisioning the outcome of the conversation before it begins, you will have a clear idea of the most suitable approach and tone. This will also keep you on track. So often people try to derail you from the topic or play games so you start losing control of the conversation. By having a clear understanding of the questions above, you can easily avoid their attempts to derail you. If you accept their invitation to redirect the conversation, you will not achieve your desired outcome. If the person makes unrelated comments that require addressing, save that for another conversation at a different time.

For example, if you need to give a team member feedback for failing to meet a deadline, the desired outcome might be that the employee understands how their actions negatively affect the team and both parties should agree on action steps to avoid it from reoccurring. What you don't want is bickering or anyone playing the blame-game. You want to walk away with a professional and respectful work relationship.

There may be occasions when you need to end a relationship or partnership, which of course will completely change what you say to the person.

> In the workshop mentioned earlier, the team members told the Director: We would like to be able to draw a line in the sand with regards to everything that has already happened. We want to start fresh so that moving forward we can ensure that the company will meet its deadlines. We want to be able to rely on team members to deliver on all of their responsibilities.
>
> What we don't want is for a "he said, she said" scenario to take place and for us to start blaming each other for what has already happened.
>
> We want to work well with you. We miss the "you" that was passionate and motivated. We need you. Let's work out a way to support you so that you can deliver on time.

Some of you may be thinking: "All I want to do is have the damn conversation why do I need to do so much reflection?" If you are leading people, it's your obligation to prepare for difficult conversations and deliver them well so that both parties feel respected. What tends to happen is that the leader dominates the conversation, lands the message loud and clear but leaves the team member with a broken ego, battered confidence and a "screw you" attitude. This will only make things worse and that is ALL ON YOU. So put in the effort, go through these steps and be a leader that gets shit done and strengthens relationships.

CHAPTER 4: *navigating tough conversations*

2 Be self-aware

It's hard to predict exactly how the conversation will go, but it's wise to plan ahead. Think about what message you want send and how the other person may react.

It's also important to consider what could trigger you. What could the other person say or do during the conversation that would evoke a response from your Critical Parent or Rebellious Child ego states? If something does upset you, what would be the best way to respond? Which triggers should you be aware of but ignore as they are simply invitations to derail the conversation. If you accept invitations for the conversation to escalate, you will only have yourself to blame.

(Remember chapter 3)

Alternatively, is there anything that you could say that could lead to an adverse response from the other person? What are the manipulative comments that you may be tempted to say when you are fearful of losing control. It isn't easy to acknowledge your triggers but if you don't identify them, you can't remove them from the conversation.

Take the time to consider these situations and write them down. By considering all of the scenarios that could play out, it will be easier to stay in control and now allow the conversation to go from constructive to to toxic.

> *Going back to the innovations team... They realised that while they could be vindictive and bring up example after example of when the Director messed up, but how would that benefit the team? Furthermore, they understood that attacking his character would hurt him, but not result in better performance. So that avoided those triggers.*
>
> *Meanwhile, the Director could have come up with a plethora of excuses for every single time he failed to perform. Alternatively, he could have activated his Free Child ego state to make jokes to lighten the mood (which is a defense strategy that he is good at) but this would not have resolved the issue.*

3 Make it a safe space

Firstly, you need to ask yourself: **DO I NEED TO APOLOGISE?** If so, get over yourself and reflect on what have you done to add fuel to the fire. Perhaps you need to say: "I have given our situation some thought and I realised that I didn't make things easy for you and for that I'm sorry."

I'm not implying that you are to blame in every scenario, but sometimes an apology for your role is a great place to start. Simply saying: "I'm really sorry we are in this situation" goes a long way.

An apology doesn't make you weak, it shows you have taken the time to reflect.

It's important that during the conversation the other person doesn't feel attacked and become defensive, as this could result in conflict.

Don't approach the person when they are stressed or flustered, or when there are other people around. It's best to arrange a time and place where you can have a private conversation. Then consider what you could say to put the person at ease. While it's important to be honest and direct, demonstrating some empathy will help to keep the conversation cordial.

> When I consulted with the innovations team prior to the workshop, they all said that the worst thing the Director did was not apologise or acknowledge the problems he caused for the team. They said that it was as if he was so thick that he just didn't get it. They didn't receive a single apology for his non-delivery and lack of productivity… nothing! When I consulted with the Director, he said: "I have shown them my remorse by agreeing to do this intervention and by trying harder. Surely they can see that I am trying to make it better."

To everyone reading this. **THAT IS NOT THE SAME AS APOLOGISING.** It just isn't. Prior to this difficult conversation, both parties had time to process and reflect on how to ensure that the conversation remained respectful and constructive and this is what was said:

> **Team:** "We realise that we tried to enforce very strict processes and procedures on you. Considering that you are an expressive personality, this must have been a total creativity killer and pushed you into your Rebellious Child ego state – and for that we apologise."
>
> **Director:** "After taking the time to reflect, I realise that trying change my behaviour is not an apology. I'm sorry for not acknowledging how my behaviour affected the team. I'm sorry for not delivering and missing deadlines and mostly I'm sorry for jeopardising our relationship as we have worked together for many years."

This came from someone who hardly ever apologises because he finds it hard. And guess what? He lived to tell the tale and the team is stronger than ever.

4 Master your own stories

As human beings, we tend to overthink and build things up in our heads. If you

CHAPTER 4: *navigating tough conversations*

label a conversation as "tough" before it even begins, it may turn out to be a self-fulfilling prophecy. Instead of worrying and allowing the situation to fester, tackle the conversation as soon as possible and approach it with a positive, open outlook.

It's crucial to reflect on what have you already told yourself about the situation you are in.

You might have negative thoughts such as:
→ *My colleagues probably think I'm an arse.*
→ *I bet they are trying to prove me wrong.*
→ *They are upset because of something that happened in the past and now they have it in for me.*
→ *They want me to fail.*
→ *He/she is already looking for a new job. I can just sense it.*
→ *He/she is a lost cause. Their performance is not going to change.*
→ *He/she hates their job.*
→ *He/she dislikes me.*

You get the idea. What stories have you told yourself about a person or situation that simply made the situation worse in your head? What's worse is that these stories are based purely on assumptions. These assumptions become beliefs, which turn into convictions. And the only thing that can come from that is a failed conversation.

For the innovations team, the stories were:
→ *The Director checked out and is only interested in fancy strategy work.*
→ *He thinks we are only capable of handling operations.*
→ *He has lost interest in the business.*

For the Director, the stories were:
→ *They are trying to control me.*
→ *They are putting all these processes in place just to piss me off and to punish me for the past.*
→ *They have it in for me. It doesn't matter what I say or what my reason is they will always find a way to make me look bad.*

Which brings out the Free Child in all of us.

The interesting thing is that when you admit these stories you demonstrate vulnerability and show the other party that you realise that your own assumptions have made things worse in your head. When people share the stories in their heads, it often leads to laughter when people realise how silly some of their stories are. Now that you have identified what you want from the conversation and reflected on the things that can support and damage this process, it's time to construct your message.

By the way, this chapter and chapter 12 are interrelated, so feel free to read it in conjunction with this one.

5. Plan and then have the conversation

And now my own network will recognise this.

First plan your opening statement. A statement that I love and often works well is:

contrasting statement → **"What I don't want is... but what I do want is..."**

Then start the difficult conversation.

There are several ways the conversation could go, so it helps to have a list of points that you will discuss. I find the D4 Feedback model by Insight Discovery super useful. It links so well to the social styles we discussed in chapter 1. I suggest approaching difficult conversations in the following way:

❶ **The facts (this speaks to analysers):** It's important to be direct and clear. Starting with the facts and giving real examples will give the conversation context and ensure that both people are on the same page. → **For example:** *"There have been several occasions where you agreed to complete a task in a meeting but when I followed up it was incomplete. This also happened on Tuesday when you missed your deadline."*

❷ **Your feelings (this speaks to amiables):** Discuss how you feel as a result of the person's actions. → **For example:** *"When you miss a deadline, it makes me frustrated because I was under the impression that everything was on track, so it was disappointing to find out that it wasn't."*

❸ **The impact (this speaks to expressives):** Discuss the impact their actions have on the team. → **For example:** *"This negatively affects the team because the other team members cannot complete the project until you meet your deadline. I know this sounds crazy, but I think that you are doing it on purpose and that you want to sabotage the team, silly right?"*

❹ **A solution (this speaks to drivers):** There is no point in having a difficult conversation if the situation isn't resolved. Discuss and agree on an action plan that will be implemented moving forward, as well as what needs to be done to ensure the situation doesn't happen again. → **For example:** *"What I would like is that you complete this task by 10 September. In the future, the moment you have doubts or concerns about meeting a deadline, please communicate this with me and don't wait for me to follow up."*

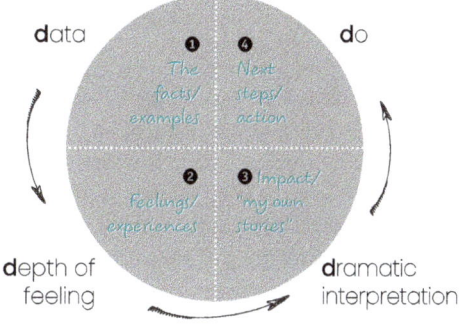

Insight Discovery's **D4** feedback model

CHAPTER 4: *navigating tough conversations*

The innovation team's conversation went something like this:

> **Contrasting statement:**
> What we don't want to happen is for us to blame each other and mess up our long-standing relationship. What we do want is to find a solution that works for all of us, and for everyone to commit to making this work.
>
> **The actual message:**
> ❶ There have been many occasions in the past when you missed deadlines, failed to log or update tickets and promised to deliver information and then four weeks later we hadn't heard from you. We requested information from you in email threads and in our ticketing system. This started happening six months ago.
>
> ❷ Initially we just let it go but it's getting to a point where we're all feeling angry with you, as well as embarrassed when we speak to clients. To be honest, we have no idea what to do anymore.
>
> *Keep in mind that the Director is an expressive so exclusion for him is a sign of rejection.*
>
> ❸ We are at the stage where we are excluding you and trying to avoid setting up projects where you may be involved. The delays we are experiencing have had a huge impact on the team and we have lost trust in your ability to deliver. We are currently questioning whether you still want to be a part of this company.
>
> ❹ Moving forward, we would like to deliver on time and be proud of our output. In order to do that, we need you to either be totally committed or consciously remove yourself from the operation so that we can start putting resources in place to replace you. We don't want the latter as your technical problem solving skills are your superpower, but we have to put the business and our clients first. If you chose the former then we also need to put processes in place in case you fall behind again.
>
> The important thing to know is that we are willing to give this one more try and give you 100% benefit of the doubt but if we go back to square one after this new agreement, we will have to raise it with to the board of directors because this is a serious situation. Of course, we hope that this will not be necessary. I know it seems like a lot to consider, but it's better than dealing with the repercussions or conflict if things don't go well.

6. Give the other person time to engage

Your conversation doesn't end here. You have to get the other person to engage and take part in what may be an intense, yet effective conversation. Encourage them to participate. It's important that they feel heard so ask them about their feelings, experiences or opinions. Also, ensure that they understand and agree to the action plan.

You can foster participation by saying the following:
→ *"Now that you have heard what I wanted to say, I would love to hear your thoughts."*
→ *"What's going through your mind now that you have heard what I wanted to say?"*
→ *"I know this isn't easy to hear but I'm dying to hear what you think or feel?"*
→ *"I'm sure you have a lot to comment on. I would love to hear what you are thinking."*

While having tough conversations are difficult, it's essential because it allows a professional relationship to grow. When you can tackle an issue head on but with respect, it increases performance and unity within a team. Many people struggle in the beginning but the more you do it, the easier it will become. It actually becomes addictive because you realise how much a relationship can grow with each tough conversation. The more you practice, the better you will become. It will reach a point where you can dive into a difficult conversation right off the cuff.

Chapter checklist

☐ Ask your teams how they rate their ability to have tough conversations on a scale of 1 to 10.
☐ Ask them to identify a specific conversation that they would like to explore. This could be one that has already happened and they want to reflect on, or a conversation that will take place.
☐ Discuss the six steps of crucial conversations.
☐ Ask team members to get into groups and discuss how the difficult conversation should unfold according to the six steps.
☐ Get people to share what they have learnt from this activity.
☐ If the conversation is yet to happen, ask them to set a deadline for the conversation.

chapter 5

Your attitude as a leader

There are many famous quotes that describe how important a good attitude is. But, having a positive attitude doesn't just mean putting a smile on your face and getting shit done. This is particularly important for people who step into a leadership position for the first time. Many new leaders fail to lead gracefully and operate with a chip on their shoulder. They manage from their Critical Parent ego state and bombard their team members with demands and expectations, which can lead the team to feel unmotivated and demoralised and negatively impact productivity.

Similarly, a leader who operates from their Adaptive Child ego state allows their team members to walk all over them, resulting in a team that doesn't take responsibility or accountability for their roles. Nobody likes a domineering boss or a pushover, so it's crucial that you strike the right balance.

There are no two ways about it. Having a positive attitude is vital for leadership success because it results in better professional relationships, productivity and collaboration. But why are some leaders so good at rallying their team in a positive way, while others struggle to gain the respect of their team members?

Eric Berne, author of *The Games People Play*, explains that a person's attitude is a manifestation of one of the four different life positions. Each one of these positions describes a way of being and are based on the level of okayness, which looks at how much you value yourself as a human being, as well as how much you value the people you interact with.

Being in a healthy life position means that you don't see yourself as better or less than the other person, but on equal footing regardless of age or rank. It's important to note that you might not always be okay with someone's actions or behaviour, but you need to maintain respect for the person you are dealing with.

Berne says that the way someone views themselves and the world is crystalised in the first five years of their life. If a person's parents or primary caregivers are encouraging and supportive, it fosters a healthy sense of self worth. While people who are criticised or ignored in their early years tend to have low self-esteem and a negative attitude. Once a person adopts a default life position, it usually remains fixed unless they put in considerable effort to change it.

Eric Berne's life positions look something like this:

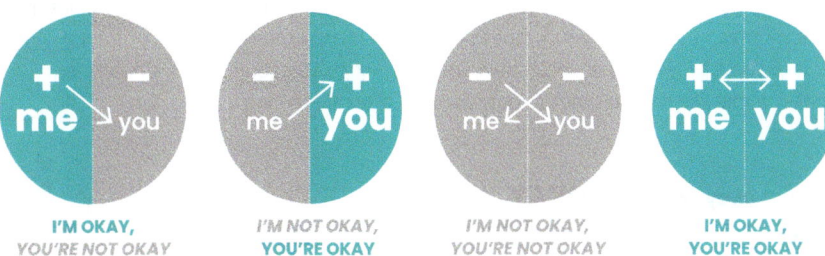

I'M OKAY,
YOU'RE NOT OKAY

I'M NOT OKAY,
YOU'RE OKAY

I'M NOT OKAY,
YOU'RE NOT OKAY

I'M OKAY,
YOU'RE OKAY

I'M OKAY, *You're not okay*

When someone is in this life position, they put themselves on a pedestal and believe that they are better than others. They look down on the person they are interacting with and see them as small or inferior. This is unhealthy because they tend to treat people that they deem as inferior with anger, disdain or disgust.

This tends to happen when people are not used to having power and it can lead to disengagement and disharmony within a team. This is particularly true, when it comes to having tough conversations because the other person may feel like they are being bulldozed and need to defend themselves.

Many of these behaviours stem from Parent ego states. When someone becomes judgmental or hostile, they are operating from Critical Parent. People in this life position don't trust people to stand on their own two feet and they feel the need to save them, which is characteristic of the Nurturing Parent state.

Common traits
→ Trying to show that you are better than others
→ Finding it difficult to delegate because you believe you do things better than others
→ Not trusting others, only trusting yourself
→ Walking all over other people
→ Being hurtful or hostile
→ Blaming people
→ Being defensive or aggressive

So many leaders I meet in team developments say to me: "I'm hardly ever in I'm okay, You're not okay". They believe that they focus on solutions and treat their team members with utter respect. However, when their team members feel like they are in a safe space, they often share some of their negative thoughts and experiences. Leaders

CHAPTER 5: *your attitude as a leader*

I'll share a personal story at the end of this chapter.

are usually surprised to hear about their team member's grievances, which means they have a blind spot. Just because your words sound like they come from a good place, it doesn't mean that that is what your team members are experiencing.

Take some time to think about how you react when someone misses a deadline, makes a mistake or is hesitant to participate in a team meeting.

I'm not okay, **YOU'RE OKAY**

People who occupy this space see themselves as small or inadequate and they look up to people they believe are superior. This doesn't mean that the person has a higher rank or is older than them, but they tend to make themselves smaller in the presence of others. They also discount their own feelings or opinions.

This is an unhealthy state because the predominant feelings are fear and sadness. It's common for people in this position to withdraw from situations or feel like the victim.

Common traits
→ Feeling anxious or nervous around other people
→ Believing that other people are better or can do something better than you
→ Constantly putting yourself down or making yourself smaller
→ Not feeling good about yourself
→ Feeling like the victim
→ Lacking self confidence
→ Blaming yourself
→ Low self esteem

I want you to spend some time reflecting here.

What are some typical things you say in meetings? Do you ever say sentences like:

"So this might be a stupid question but…"

"I'm not sure if this is a great idea but let me put it out there in any case…"

Just using this type of language demonstrates your frame of mind. When you are in an unhealthy position you invite the other party to view you as NOT okay. And then you are surprised when they don't listen to you or respect you.

Stop sending out the invitation!

I'm not okay, You're not okay
This is the worst life position to occupy because it feels like a place of hopelessness or depression. A person in this position sees themselves, as well as others as small or inadequate. There is no winning recipe here. They have lost interest in life and often feel like they cannot cope in the real world, which can be dangerous and lead to destructive behaviour such as extreme withdrawal or violence.

Common traits
→ Unable to find solutions to problems
→ Feeling like no one, including yourself, is good enough
→ Living in a state of depression
→ Viewing yourself as unlovable. Creating a space where no one can get through to you
→ Rejecting ideas and other people
→ Feeling hopeless
→ Having no trust in yourself or others

Spending too much time in this life position can lead to depression because you feel like there is no hope, which can lead to clinical issues that go way beyond this book. Everyone has low points in their lives and it's important to talk about and get out of this state as quickly as possible.

It can be very hard to go from *I'm not okay; You're not okay* to a healthy state. My suggestion is to focus on getting to the next level of okayness by working on ways to improve your current mindset. This is a very good time to step into your Adult ego state. Consider what you can and can't control and implement steps to make your world a positive place. *Which we will analyse further in chapter 11.*

I'M OKAY, YOU'RE OKAY

This is a healthy life position because this is when a person has the ability to see themselves and others as completely equal. They believe that their life has value and they are worthy. They are accepting of others, do not place blame and have a "can do" attitude.

This is the life position that all individuals should strive for. When leaders operate from this space, it's rewarding for team members because they feel heard and valued. They aren't afraid of tough conversations because they have the ability to ensure that both parties walk away feeling respected.

This is the position where the cliché "tackle the issue not the person" is very apt. In this healthy position you are able to deal with the person with respect but deal with workplace issues such as a team member's mistake, discussions about performance, and issues related to tardiness, lying or hiding.

Common traits
→ Willing to explore and look for solutions to problems
→ Not dwelling on things. Always looking at ways to move forward
→ The ability to see opportunities for growth
→ Viewing yourself and others positively
→ Not shying away from issues. Having the ability to discuss and tackle issues head on
→ An ability to communicate in a way that leaves everyone feeling respected

The bitter pill I had to swallow

> Years ago when I was in my early 30s, I was working at my previous company and had an amazing team. However, I started feeling like people were tiptoeing around me and I always sensed tension when I was in the office. Needless to say, I was under a lot of pressure. I had to lead a team, while dealing with one business partner who was making my life hell by not performing, while the other one was smashing her role out of the park. I also had to focus on scaling the business while I was pregnant with twins.
>
> I decided to do a quick 360-degree survey. I needed to know what was going on and if the issue was me. *Which was self designed and self administered, nothing fancy*
>
>
>
> **The survey included the following questions:**
> → What about my leadership style is working for you?
> → What is difficult for you?
> → What would you like me to stop, start and continue doing?
> → If you could say anything to help me grow, what would that be? (This is the question that generated the juicy stuff that was so hard to swallow).
>
> *reality dosage: take often*
>
> So Shafieka Moos, the absolute best Personal Assistant and Office Manager I ever had, said to me: *Sadly I couldn't take her with me when I left the company*
>
> "Heléne, you are amazing and what you say is well thought through, but what your face says and what you actually say are two very different things. You sometimes come across as just a downright BITCH but I love you."

This is a sentence that I share when I work with team to this day. It was so hard to read and at first I wanted to strangle her, but then I realised I just received the best gift any leader could ever ask for: **direct and honest feedback.** That statement changed who I fundamentally am as a person and as a leader.

I urge you to be honest with yourself, when you are not in *I'm okay, You're okay.* Where do you lead from and what impact does this have on the people you are leading? Step up and lead, don't hide behind a life position. You are better than that.

It happens to all of us – don't bullshit yourself

How to move out of a negative life position

Getting the best out of yourself and your team starts with acknowledging your default life position. Remember that no one operates from a healthy position 100% of the time. It's common to move into an unhealthy space in times of stress. For example, I often shift into *I'm not okay, You're okay* when I'm in a situation where I think someone knows more than me. I also go into *I'm okay, You're not okay* when I'm frustrated with someone who isn't doing a task to the standard that I expect, or worse when they ask me the same thing twice. Now I say to myself: "I obviously didn't make myself clear enough. Let's try this again." Then I make a real effort.

It gets me every time.

While it's perfectly normal to move into a negative life position at times, you should make an effort to operate from *I'm okay, You're okay* the majority of the time. If you find yourself in a negative space, follow these steps:

→ **Identify which life position you are in.** Consider what emotion you are feeling. Is it anger, worry, sadness or something else?
→ **Identify where the problem lies.** Do you need to gain okayness within yourself or within others?
→ **Consider what triggered you to move into the negative space.** This could be something in your environment, a stressful situation or a particular person. Try to avoid the triggers that have a negative effect on you.
→ **Determine what you can do to move out of the negative mindset.** Failure to do so means operating in an uncomfortable work environment and nobody functions at their best when the office is miserable. Try to fix the situation as soon as you can. Then draw up a list of action steps that you can implement to move into *I'm okay, You're okay.* I often ask: "What story am I telling myself and how true is that story?" The following steps may be helpful.

CHAPTER 5: your attitude as a leader

If you're in the life position...

I'M OKAY, You're not okay

→ Learn to see the value in other people. Tell people when they do something that you appreciate or admire.
→ Remember that you aren't perfect. Everyone has flaws and so do you, so stop seeing yourself as superior to others.
→ Contemplate the source of your anger or frustration. What are your triggers and how can you avoid them?
→ When you feel angry, learn to talk through issues rather than becoming aggressive or violent.
→ Talk to someone you trust or find a professional to work through your past or issues that you haven't dealt with.
→ Learn to trust people.
→ Find healthy ways to relieve stress such as exercise, yoga or meditation.
→ Try saying this sentence: "I must admit I'm quite angry but let's set that aside and see how we can fix this and then we can discuss how to avoid this from happening again."

Which is one of my personal favourites

I'm not okay, YOU'RE OKAY

→ Take the time to appreciate the value that you add to the world. Write a list of your positive attributes.
→ Seek and nurture positive relationships. Surround yourself with people who are supportive and genuine.
→ Practice asking people for help.
→ Learn to trust people mindfully.
→ Practice appreciation.
→ Monitor your thoughts and when negative thoughts creep in, say positive affirmations.
→ Speak to someone that knows you well and that knows that you go into this space. Use this person as a soundboard to reflect on your thoughts and dispel your assumptions. This should be a space where you can be honest about why you don't feel okay and you can work through the issue together. For me, this person is one of my team members. You can speak to a coach or a therapist, but I find that having someone that is readily available is so much better.

This is my favourite way to move into a healthy life position

I'm not okay, You're not okay

→ If you feel depressed or hopeless, seek professional help. People see this as a weakness and want to avoid it but at Credo Growth we see this as essential and as a strength. If someone tells me they are in therapy or they have a coach or a counselor, my respect level for them increases instantaneously. It means that they are not afraid to dig deep, reflect, learn and grow. I'd even go as far as saying that if you feel this is beneath you, you may not be ready to lead yet so step aside so that someone with guts can.
→ Consider the source of your unhappiness and hopelessness. Once you identify the trauma, take steps to heal.
→ Foster healthy, positive relationships. Spend time with people who leave you feeling good about yourself.
→ Take stock of the good things in your life and practice appreciation.
→ Be mindful of your thoughts. Practice visualisation to help cultivate positive feelings and thoughts.

Using this knowledge will take your team from good to incredible. Share these insights with your team to help them gain an understanding about how they view themselves, as well as the world. This is invaluable because operating from an unhealthy life position can result in discomfort and conflict for yourself and for those around you, which leads to mediocrity and no one wants that.

Ask each team member to identify their default position. Put masking tape on the floor and create a quadrant for each position. Encourage team members to step into the quadrant of their default position. Ask them to be honest and discuss what it looks like to be in a healthy and an unhealthy position. How does this affect them as individuals, as well as the team?

Then ask team members to consider which life position they adopt when they are stressed or when the pressure is on. It's very normal for people to shift to a negative space when they are taking strain. Have a discussion as to why the shift occurs and how it affects their own and the team's performance. Then discuss how individuals can deal with those scenarios and what can be done to move back to *I'm okay, You're okay.*

Ask the team to consider the collaboration agreements discussed in Chapter 1. Then discuss what the team can do to ensure that each person operates from the *I'm okay, You're okay* box. Having these discussions can help each person improve their attitude in the workplace and in life.

Chapter checklist

☐ Discuss the four different life positions with your team.
☐ Determine your default life position.
☐ Consider when you move into a negative life position. What triggers you?
☐ What action steps can you take to move back into *I'm okay, You're okay?*
☐ Ask teammates to identify their default position. Discuss and explore.
☐ Ask people to identify which position they operate from when they are under pressure or a crisis happens?
☐ How does that impact them as individuals, as well as the team?
☐ Discuss what triggers them to move into that state.
☐ What steps can they take to move into a healthy life position?
☐ Ask the team to consider what they think the team's life position is and if it is serving the team. If not, what can the team do it change it? 💬

chapter 6
Lead like a coach

Gone are the days where leaders can just bark orders at their employees and expect them to deliver. In today's competitive business landscape, leaders need to grow some balls, patience and have a real interest in their people to develop their team. The most effective way to achieve greatness for your team is through coaching. Not only does it improve team member's skills, it fosters an environment of independence, problem solving and collaboration. Other benefits include increased employee engagement and job satisfaction and higher productivity for the entire team.

And high productivity means no mediocrity!

According to a study conducted by the International Coach Federation, 75% of business leaders believe that coaching is an integral part of a team's success, yet only 25% of organisations have a strong coaching culture. So why the heck are so many businesses failing to implement coaching?

Many leaders see it as an unnecessary time waster. However, I have found a very practical and effective model that is suitable for all kinds of scenarios. The GROW approach developed by Sir John Whitmore, author of the book *Coaching for Performance*, can be utilised for intense coaching sessions that last an hour or for quick sessions in the corridor when someone needs help navigating a task.

The steps outlined in the model are ideal to add to your arsenal of tools for when you need to engage with your team members. It's a great way to get the team to think, tackle problem solving and improve their confidence. Very often people confuse coaching with giving advice or mentorship. However, it's about guiding people through a set of questions to help them find solutions.

G.R.O.W. (Goal, **R**eality, **O**ptions, **W**ill or **W**ay Forward) is a simple four-step process that focuses on unlocking the coachee's inner reflection, learning and problem solving. As Whitmore says in the book: "Coaching is about unlocking a person's potential to maximise their own performance. You need to help them to learn rather than teach them."

The most important aspect of a successful coaching session is that you cannot go into it with an ego. Coaching is not about what you want or think, it's all about the coachee. When you start a session, stop what you are doing and give 100% of your focus to your team member because guiding them through their own thinking and problem-solving requires you to be present.

Leaders often say to me: "When I coached my team members, it didn't work."
When I ask them how they coach, I usually get one of the following responses:

→ *I tell them exactly how to do a task and they still get it wrong.*
→ *I show them how to do things.*
→ *I tell them where they went wrong.*
→ *I share my experiences.*
→ *I give them advice on what they should do.*

Guess what? None of what is described above constitutes as coaching.

Coaching is hard if you are a leader or a manager and it will take some time and practice to get it right. But once you get the hang of it and do it often it's amazing to see how your team starts to develop and grow and become more engaged. It does, however, require practice and perseverance from your side.

We work with many clients where we act as external coaches and we coach both the leaders and the team members and you can clearly see the development that takes place. What we do is equip leaders with tools and coaching skills so that they can get the best out of their people. This chapter aims to share what we normally do over four days of training. Combine this with everything you learn in this book, and you will be on your way to becoming an amazing coach for your team.

GOAL
The first step of any coaching session is to agree on a topic.

> Once I made the mistake of making assumptions during a coaching session. My assistant asked me for help with the financials and I immediately jumped in without asking her any questions. I looked at it, identified the mistake and gave it back to her. She had the guts to inform me that she just wanted me to check something so she could figure it out for herself. This wouldn't have happened if I had taken the time to gauge what she needed from me, instead of bulldozing my way through the process.

Don't try to be the hero in every situation! By assuming that you need to bail out your employee or do their work for them, you are robbing them of an opportunity to learn and grow. At the beginning of every coaching session, ask questions to determine exactly what they hope to achieve through the session and what the coachee requires from you as their

CHAPTER 6: *lead like a coach*

leader. Do they need you to challenge them, motivate them or guide them through a process? Agree on a topic and determine specific objectives for the session and do not go off track.

> **Questions to ask**
> → *What would you like to discuss?*
> → *What do you want to achieve in this session?*
> → *What exactly do you need from me?*
> → *Do you need help? If so, what kind of help?*
> → *What would you like to see happen after this session?*

The easiest way to tell that the goal isn't clear is when you, as the coach, feel like you are running in circles and not having a concrete discussion. Always go back and focus on the goal if your session is dragging.

2 REALITY

It's important to unpack the coachee's position and really understand what they are dealing with. This is my favourite stage because you get to ask them a plethora of questions and give them the time to digest, reflect and understand where they stand in regards to the problem they are facing. It's a journey of self-assessment and self-awareness. Ask questions to get the person to reflect on the challenges they are facing and the potential way forward. It's also important to check and dispel assumptions. This is the most time consuming part of any coaching session.

> **Questions to ask**
> → *What about this is difficult for you?*
> → *How often does this occur?*
> → *What impact or effect does this have?*
> → *Are there other factors that are relevant?*
> → *If you had a friend in the same scenario, what advice would you offer them?*
> → *When is this not the case?*
> → *What have you done or tried to date?*
> → *What are you doing to make the situation worse?*
> → *What is stopping you from dealing with this?*
> → *What does your gut say about this?*

Many leaders don't spend enough time in the reality phase. We are solution-driven machines and spending time in reality means that there are no solutions, no quick fixes, no advice or giving instructions. *This is the frustrating part for most leaders.*

Get this, if you give people solutions in this phase, you are telling them that you don't believe they can come up with their own solutions. This comes from an *I'm okay, You're not okay space,* as well as your Parent (both Critical or Nurturing) ego state. You are also depriving them of a learning opportunity by skipping the reality phase and moving on to your options or solutions. STOP being selfish, it's not about you it's about the coachee.

3 OPTIONS

Once the coachee has taken the time to reflect, prompt them to suggest ideas to address their problem. This is the time to go wild and suggest the wackiest, off the wall solutions... nothing is off limits. Then encourage them to evaluate the pros and cons of each option. It's all about getting them to gauge all the options available to them. It's important not to make a choice for the person. The coachee learns by weighing up the possibilities and making a choice for themselves.

> **Questions to ask**
> → *What have you tried so far?*
> → *Which ideas do you think won't work?*
> → *If you had a friend in this situation, what advice would you give them?*
> → *What would you like to do or try?*
> → *What alternatives are there?*
> → *Who might be able to help you?*
> → *What is the wackiest idea that you have but have been too scared to implement?*
> → *Can you identify the pros and cons of that option?*
> → *Do you have a preferred option?*

I'll say again: **it's about them, not you!**

They might come up with ideas that you don't like but could still work. What may happen is that the coachee comes up with an idea that is against company policy or isn't physically possible in the current working environment. In this case, you could ask questions such as:

→ *Do you think this is really something that could work in our business?*
→ *With the current policies in place, is that a viable idea?*
→ *What obstacles would you face if you implemented this idea?*

Please don't skip this phase. I have seen time and time again how this phase energises team members. They are proud of the ideas they come up with and are eager to execute them. The excitement isn't as great when it isn't their own idea.

CHAPTER 6: *lead like a coach*

4 WILL OR WAY FORWARD

The final step is getting commitment from the coachee. It's important for them to outline what they will do moving forward. Get them to draw up a list of detailed action steps, as well as a time frame for each one. Agree on what kind of support you will offer and determine if you will have a follow up coaching session. Ask the coachee to identify potential obstacles and then discuss how they will be overcome should they arise. Lastly, offer them a word of encouragement. Tap in your Nurturing Parent and tell them that you know that they can do it.

> **Questions to ask**
> → What is the option that you feel will work best for right now?
> → What are your next steps?
> → What is your time frame?
> → Can you anticipate anything getting in your way?
> → How will you track your progress?
> → What support might you need?
> → How and when can you get that support?

Something that most leaders really enjoy is the action plan – and this phase is exactly that. After going through a lot of processing and reflection, it's time to determine the next steps. Make sure that you get the coachee to commit to completing the action plan by a set deadline. As a leader, also encourage the team member to arrange a follow up chat with you to discuss progress on the outcome of their actions.

A summary of Sir John Whitemore's GROW approach to coaching

GOAL	**R**EALITY	**O**PTIONS	**W**ILL/ **W**AY FORWARD
→ Agree on a topic	→ Spend time unpacking	→ Explore all ideas and options	→ What will you do?
→ What would you like to achieve?	→ Journey of self assessment	→ Think creatively	→ Details/specifics
→ What do you need?	→ What is the current situation?	→ What could you do to move forward?	→ What support do you need?
	→ Check assumptions/ stories	→ Encourage	→ Encourage

50

HOW TO COACH EFFECTIVELY

You might think that coaching requires a lot of time and effort but I just want to remind you that every time you give someone the experience of coaching, their engagement increases because they are using their own brainpower to come up with solutions. And soon you will find that people will start to make decisions on their own before they come to you. So essentially, you're helping them to formulate a new way of thinking so that they can find their own solutions in the future. People who can make their own decisions are more time efficient and work more confidently. That's ultimately what you want as a leader.

While coaching is an effective tool to empower your team, it doesn't always come naturally to leaders. If you or your team are not accustomed to coaching sessions, it may feel awkward at first but the more you do it, the more comfortable and collaborative the team will become. I have devised six steps for you to follow to make your coaching sessions more effective and seamless:

1 > Listen, reflect, question and repeat

Have you ever been in a scenario where someone came to you for advice, and they talked and talked and talked? At the end they said they felt much better and they thanked you for your help but you didn't actually say much. This is because more often than not people are capable of finding their own solutions, they just need someone to listen to them and time to process their own thoughts.

The best formula for any coaching session is to listen. As the coach, you are there to ask questions and give the coachee the time and space to process. When you ask a question, it's about really listening to what the person is saying when they answer you. Then rephrase what they said because this gives them time to reflect and offers you a chance to check whether you understood. Then ask them another question or a follow up question. And repeat.

We also tackle listening in chapter 10 where we look at three levels of listening.

2 > Offer guidance, not advice

It's so tempting to tell people what to do but remember coaching is not about you or your opinions! In fact, the most difficult aspect of coaching is not giving advice or offering solutions because that will simply force your own ideas on the coachee.

Stay away from phrases that aim to guide or instruct such as:	Instead ask coaching questions like:
"Have you tried…?"	*"What have you tried?"*
"You should…"	*"What are you thinking of doing?"*
"Why don't you…"	*"What do you think is the best solution?"*
"What about…"	*"Which ideas have you already vetoed?"*

3 > **The solution is not your responsibility**

Remember that you are there to guide the coachee through their thinking, not to give them a solution. If the coach makes the final decision, it's selfish because you have different personalities and you operate in different environments so your solution may not fit them.

Don't rob the coachee of the opportunity to work through a problem and make a decision. It may be difficult but take a step back because it isn't your circus or your animals. Remember that when coachees are encouraged to think for themselves, they will reach a stage where they are able to tackle problems alone, which will improve productivity for both parties.

4 > **Don't give more energy than the coachee**

During the coaching session, if you feel like you're giving more energy than the coachee, then you probably aren't in coaching mode. This could mean that you're in instruction mode or that you've taken on the coachee's problems, which doesn't provide them with a platform for learning.

While it's your job to guide the coachee, they have to put in the work. Always ensure that the majority of the energy and engagement comes from them. The moment you feel that you are struggling to come up with a solution you are expending too much energy. Your energy should be spent on listening, reflecting and questioning.

5 > **Use your gut**

I've been in many coaching sessions where I raised a concern or asked a question and the coachee responded by saying that that's not what they meant or a specific question doesn't apply to them. Don't feel guilty just because some of the questions don't apply or aren't effective. Even those questions can be a reflection tool. Just move on and use your intuition as a tool for probing. Always trust your gut.

If a question comes up while you are coaching there's a reason for it, so ask the question. The sentences that I use in such cases are:

→ *"Something just occurred to me. I'm not sure why but I'm going to ask it anyway..."*
→ *"I felt my mind going in a different direction when you said..."*
→ *"This might not be relevant, but..."*

6 > **Practice, practice, practice**

It takes time to develop a coaching culture, so don't try and rush it or the results will be rushed. The more coaching sessions you lead, the more questions you'll have at hand. Metaphors are also an effective way to connect. For example, if the coachee says their ship is sinking, stay with that and ask them if their ship is in deep or shallow waters. What is pulling them down? What is the ship made of?

You may feel inclined to introduce other elements such as flipcharts or visuals into your sessions. Visit http://bit.ly/guidingaction where you will find lots of tools at your disposal. I have posted two coaching demonstrations, one short and one more detailed session with one of my team members, so you can see how to put this model into practice.

Chapter checklist

- ☐ Identify individuals in your team that you can practice coaching with.
- ☐ Determine which areas of their roles they can improve on and in what way they would benefit from coaching. Ask them what they think so that they can indicate where they feel they can improve.
- ☐ Ask them if they are willing to participate in a coaching session with you.
- ☐ Follow the GROW model.
- ☐ Practice.
- ☐ Conduct feedback and progress follow-up sessions where necessary.

chapter 7

How to motivate your team

When you are in a leadership role, things don't always go as planned. Imagine a situation where you carefully select each of your team members and you take the necessary steps to train and coach them, but for whatever reason the team just isn't performing. You find that your star performer is no longer smashing their targets. Perhaps there are signs of sloppiness, laziness and a lack of creativity from team members. On paper the team is awesome but in reality they are simply going through the motions. This may be a sign that your team is lacking motivation.

It's not uncommon for an employee to get bored in their job, especially if they have been in the same role for several years. Productivity can decline when team members lose the desire or belief that they can add value and improve. The good news is that there are steps you can take as a leader to light a fire under their bums – and yours!

The Motivational Hungers model also falls under the theory of transactional analysis by psychiatrist Eric Berne. It's very different to the old "carrot and stick" method of motivating people. While you can't directly control a person's interest or attitude to work, this model outlines how you can create an environment that helps them to become more intrinsically motivated.

According to Berne, the source of each person's intrinsic motivation differs. There are three motivational hungers: structure, acknowledgment and stimulus. By understanding what makes both you and your team tick it will be easier to foster an environment that unlocks everyone's best. With time you will also be able to get team members to take responsibility for their own motivation.

MOTIVATIONAL HUNGERS

1 Structure

People who are motivated by structure seek orientation and security. They thrive on regularity and orderliness. To do their best, they need clear goals or tasks, as well as routine processes.

Employees who are driven by structure tend to have organised desks. They are keen to relook at things and put plans and processes in place. They need to know exactly what is expected of them so they will ask for a clear scope. If a company lacks direction or proper protocols, they will feel overwhelmed and their motivation will decline.

Perhaps you've heard a team member say that they organised their desk or filing cabinet and they feel much better; or maybe your colleague has asked to revisit the agenda. These are indicators that they are in need of structure.

2 Acknowledgement

Team members who are driven by acknowledgment need to be recognised for their actions. They enjoy working in a team and they thrive on giving and receiving feedback. This doesn't mean that they need their colleagues to constantly sing their praises but they do need to be seen as competent. They need to be told that they are doing their tasks well and if they aren't performing they prefer to be informed. They really appreciate being on the receiving end of a warm smile.

Such employees are easy to spot because they love being involved and connecting with people so they often talk about their families or share stories. They value team spirit so they try to foster it in their team. If a team member is motivated by acknowledgment but doesn't receive feedback, their motivation and engagement are likely to drop. Also, working alone or remotely may be challenging because they are less inclined to feel appreciated.

> *I was working with an executive team where the decision was made not to include one of the senior managers in specific operational discussions to free up some of his time. This was a collective decision so there was nothing sinister about it. However, the senior manager's productivity started to decrease and several issues related to his performance began to surface. Then the Covid-19 pandemic forced the team to work remotely and the situation got worse.*
>
> *We did a motivation session with the team focusing on the three hungers. What emerged is that the senior manager felt isolated. His highest psychological need is acknowledgement and he simply didn't feel like he was a part of the team due to the lockdown and social distancing, which really affected his motivation.*
>
> *Once we talked this through the team came up with some really amazing ideas to create an environment where he could show up motivated. This included having weekly team huddles, small executive team dinners, a one-on-one meeting with the CEO and a feedback loop to ensure that he felt included. It was incredible to see how his performance started improving and how he found a new zest for the business.*

CHAPTER 7: *how to motivate your team*

3 Stimulus

This is someone who enjoys new challenges, whether they are mental or physical. For example, if they lose a client they'll try to win them back. They are always looking for an incentive, but this isn't necessarily in the form of money. They thrive on the exhilaration that comes from achieving a new goal or making the impossible possible. They are always game to try something new because it gives them energy.

You can identify such teammates because they enjoy talking about their successes, especially in business and sports. They have a tendency to try new sports or hobbies. They relish being challenged by their colleagues and often say statements such as "Watch me. I'll do it!"

The risk for a team is that if such a person is required to do the same tasks for a period of time they could become complacent and bored.

ERIC BERNE'S MOTIVATIONAL HUNGERS

Structure	Acknowledgement	Stimulus
Seeks orientation and security	*Needs to feel valued and recognised*	*Is driven by various incentives*
• Regularity	• Works well in a team	• Needs new challenges
• Clear goals/tasks	• Craves feedback	• Keen to win over clients
• Orderliness	• Needs to be seen as competent	• Goal driven
• Routine processes	• Appreciates receiving a smile	• Tries to make the impossible possible
→ Clear desk		
→ Enjoys planning	→ Speaks about family	→ Speaks about success in business/sport
→ Needs time to plan and prepare	→ Focuses on team spirit	→ Up to try something new
	→ Enjoys being involved	→ Loves proving people wrong

Stereotyping, I know

Let's take a look at how this would apply to sales people. This example demonstrates how you could use money to incentivise team members based on the three motivational hungers.

→ **If they are motivated by structure,** you could give them a higher basic salary and lower commission because they need to know exactly how much they will earn each month to feel in control.

→ **If they are motivated by** acknowledgment, you could give them a bonus and write a complimentary note such as: "This is to say thank you for smashing your targets".
→ **If they are motivated by** stimulus, you could give them a low basic salary but a very lucrative commission structure because they are driven by challenges and this would push themselves to see how much can they get.

How to increase your team's motivation
The first step to creating a motivated team is to understand what drives you. Many leaders make the mistake of encouraging their team based on their own motivational hunger. If you are motivated by structure, you are more likely to lead structurally but if your team member is motivated by stimulus this will cause their motivation to dwindle. To prevent this from happening, start by completing your hunger profile by looking at the graph below.

I'm so guilty of this.

1 → *Consider how much structure, acknowledgment and stimulus* **you prefer,** *based on your current role and plot it out on the graph.*
2 → *Contemplate how much of each of the motivational hungers* **your company or work environment provides you with** *and plot it on the graph in a different colour.*

Then analyse your graph and determine whether your current work environment is tapping into your motivational hunger. If not, what can you do to address it? For example, at the moment my current role is providing me with too much stimulus so what I can do is hire someone to manage the growth of the business. I could also read one less book a month to free up some time. To improve on acknowledgment, I could attend networking events to connect and engage with people in the industry and I could spend time recognising the efforts of individuals within the team. Lastly, to address the gap in structure, I could find ways to improve processes that are lacking in the business. It's all about taking responsibility as a leader and finding ways to ensure that I show up motivated.

The next step is to consider what makes each of your team members tick. Take the time to complete a motivational hunger profile for each person. There may be some assumptions, but do it based on what you know about them. For example, you may recognise that a team member values structure and acknowledgement but she struggles when there is too much stimulus. Therefore, it would be beneficial to give her clear directions, manage expectations and recognise when she does great work. However, it would be best not to give her too many new goals or challenges to prevent her from feeling overwhelmed.

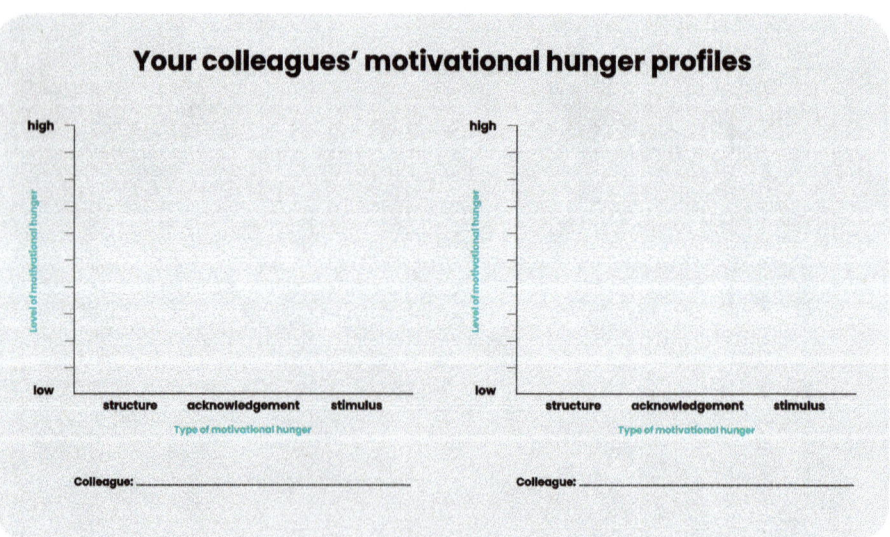

It's important to discuss motivational hungers with the team. Ask each of them to rate on a scale of 0-10 how motivated they are currently. Then explain the three motivational hungers and ask each person to do their own motivational profile.

The final step is to have a one-on-one meeting with each teammate. Together look at their motivational hunger profiles and identify which areas require some work. Ask each individual to identify ways to ensure that they are receiving the right balance of structure, acknowledgment and stimulus. This will allow employees to take ownership of their own motivation so that they can show up engaged and raring to go.

It's also important to determine what they are getting from you as a leader. Ask them to be honest and tell you what you are giving them enough of and which areas could be improved upon. You need to step up to ensure that you are motivated and that you create a space for your team to show up and get shit done!

And don't take it personally!

> 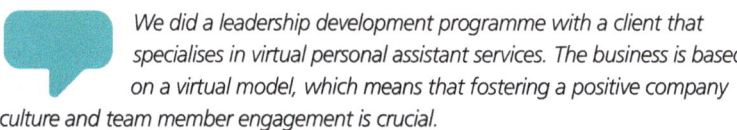 We did a leadership development programme with a client that specialises in virtual personal assistant services. The business is based on a virtual model, which means that fostering a positive company culture and team member engagement is crucial.
>
> The team leaders facilitated motivational hunger workshops with their team and they found that team members became more engaged. There were high participation rates in the monthly meetings, which were not compulsory. The project leaders said there was a positive shift in the intrinsic motivation of team members.

And that is what leaders should strive for. **It isn't only your responsibility to motivate the entire team,** everyone in your business is responsible to show up motivated. However, you do need to create an environment where this is possible.

Chapter checklist

- ☐ Complete your own motivational hunger profile.
- ☐ Identify the gaps and ways that you can improve, then write down specific action steps that you can take. And implement them!
- ☐ Do a motivational graph for each team member and get them to identify their own gaps and steps to address the gaps.
- ☐ Get each member to draw up an action plan to lessen the gaps and make this part of the weekly check-ins. Do a quick 30-second update to see how things are going.
- ☐ Determine how you can create a space for team members to be more motivated.

chapter 8

Creating a safe work environment

Have you ever had a question or idea in a business meeting but you just didn't feel comfortable or confident enough to express it? Or perhaps you have experienced working with a monster boss or worked in a nightmare company. What these situations have in common is that an asshole leader, who doesn't prioritise the safety of their team members, caused you to feel stressed or uneasy. And that is NOT okay!

While it may seem obvious that a work environment needs to be a safe place, many leaders neglect to consider the psychological safety of their employees. So often I hear team members in various teams explain that they are scared to speak up or offer ideas in the boardroom or in meetings.

And then these leaders question why engagement and motivation are low!

While I was writing this chapter I had a discussion with a potential client who asked me to put together a proposal for increasing psychological safety. She said: "Our leaders tell team members that they can speak to them about anything. However, in the majority of the exit interviews team members say that their leader bit their head off when they expressed their opinion or made a mistake."

So I want you to consider: how often do you say "my door is always open" or "mistakes are learning opportunities" but when a mistake is made you lose your cool?

Or yes, you can just Google it

There is a brilliant Ted Talk called *Building a Psychologically Safe Workplace*, by author Amy Edmondson, which is available on the Credo online course platform. In the talk, she explains that an unsafe environment is when a team member believes that they may be punished or humiliated for expressing their ideas, questions or concerns, or for making mistakes.

She adds that ensuring that your employees feel psychologically safe is crucial because it leads to more engagement, creativity and innovation. It also lowers rates of absenteeism, reduces stress and decreases turnover costs. In fact, if team members do not feel safe enough to make a mistake or speak up when something is wrong it could have devastating consequences.

In the book *Black Box Thinking: The Surprising Truth About Success,* author Matthew Syed says it's incredibly important to create an environment where team members feel confident asking questions. He describes a scenario where nurses in a hospital were too afraid to speak up and raise their concerns with a doctor when they were in an operating room and something went drastically wrong. Syed explains that there is an element of blame culture in the healthcare industry. When a surgeon makes a mistake it isn't openly addressed, which means that the same mistake could occur again.

The aviation industry, however, has a very different attitude towards failure. The sector has created a climate where it's safe to fail, which is referred to as "black box thinking". Pilots confront, document and report mistakes so that the industry can learn from them. When a pilot makes a mistake it is seen as an opportunity to improve safety. So when one pilot succeeds it isn't seen as just the individual's success, but a culmination of the failures and lessons of all the pilots involved. This is why it's so important that team members respect – not fear – their leader!

Edmondson has created a model that explains the different levels of safety teams experience. The level of psychological safety experienced depends on two factors.

→ **The first is support.** Team members should feel confident that their colleagues or leader won't have a go at them if they slip up.

→ **The second factor is accountability,** which boils down to how much people are being challenged. Employees need to feel stimulated in their roles and they need to know that if they don't deliver that they will be held accountable.

Teams generally settle into one of four safety states with varying degrees of support and accountability. As you go through them, consider where your team members are and what kind of environment are you creating as their leader.

AMY EDMONDSON'S PSYCHOLOGICAL SAFETY MODEL

support/psychological safety (low → high)		
	comfort zone → Enjoy working with each other → Not challenged → Don't work very hard	**learning zone** → Learn from mistakes → Think ahead → Willing to have difficult conversations → Focus on collaboration
	apathy zone → Uninterested → Need to be favoured → Don't share ideas	**anxiety zone** → Too afraid to talk → Too afraid to raise concerns → Scared to ask for help

accountability/challenge (low → high)

CHAPTER 8: *creating a safe environment*

1 **The comfort zone**
When team members receive a high level of psychological support but there is a low level of accountability or challenge, they settle into the comfort zone. This is when there is a routine, as well as a sense of familiarity and predictability. Team members enjoy working together and they interact often but they don't work very hard. Family-run businesses may settle in this zone because they tend to tiptoe around each other instead of holding each other accountable.

This may not feel like a bad place to be, but when employees are not being challenged they may not give it their all. It's not a place that is conducive to high engagement and creativity because the motivational hunger for stimulus is not being met.

Not to mention high performance!

2 **The apathy zone**
This isn't a good state for a team because this is when there is a low level of psychological support and very little accountability. When team members don't feel challenged or supported, they may start to wonder why they should even bother.

You may have encountered a team member like this. Someone who has a negative attitude and it seems like they are rocking up just for a paycheck. He or she isn't necessarily a bad employee, the problem is that their leader isn't giving them a reason to care. This can result in a state of chaos for the team, because individuals in a state of apathy only focus on their own needs. There is a desire to be favoured and they aren't willing to share information, which could negatively affect productivity and performance.

3 **The anxiety zone**
This is a very difficult and dangerous position to be in because team members experience a high level of accountability but there is very little psychological support. Employees are too scared to speak up or raise concerns and they fear asking for help from their leader or their colleagues. This is a scary place for them because they are overly challenged but they don't feel supported.

This state is emotionally draining and often results in disengagement, low motivation and an increase in absenteeism. While this happens in extreme cases, there are more subtle forms of workplace anxiety such as when an employee is intimidated by a colleague or leader so they avoid speaking up. They might not always show it but they may be internalising it.

In Edmondson's Ted Talk, she explains that when someone is experiencing anxiety in the workplace, it can manifest itself in many ways:

→ They don't want to be seen as ignorant, so they don't ask questions.
→ They don't want to be seen as incompetent, so they don't admit mistakes or suggest better ways of doing things.
→ They don't want to be seen as intrusive so they don't offer ideas.
→ They don't want to be seen as negative so they don't challenge the way things are.

4 The learning zone

Teams in this space receive enough psychological support and there is a healthy level of accountability and challenge. This is a great environment for team members because mistakes aren't seen as doom and gloom. Team members are open to learning from their mistakes and figuring out ways to improve things.

The team also looks ahead and predicts what can go wrong and then analyses how obstacles can be overcome. They are open to having difficult discussions and are happy to share information and ideas because they realise that they are more likely to be successful as a team than as individuals. Teams in the learning zone are comfortable asking questions, admitting mistakes, offering ideas or challenging the status quo.

I consulted with a travel business where the leader of the business was anxious about holding an incredibly sensitive team member accountable because she was worried that she would resign. She did great work and had been with the business for years so she saw her as an integral part of the company and didn't want to lose her. So the employee settled into the comfort zone and what example did the leader set for the rest of the team? That mediocrity is okay. This became extremely frustrating for some of the other team members who wanted to move to high performance. Think about it, are you letting people get away with not delivering just because you feel anxious about confronting them?

I worked with a large team in the automotive industry and I did in depth research as to why the team was stuck in the storming phase. The responses in the interviews included: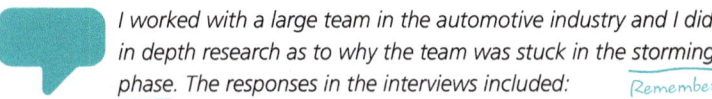
➔ *"I just come to work to do my job."*
➔ *"I don't engage because I don't trust my colleagues."*
➔ *"I don't trust that my leader as my back."*
➔ *"My teammates will backstab me to look good."*
Based on these comments, you can clearly see that there is NO psychological safety. We started an 18-month programme to deal with these issues and focus on increasing psychological safety. It entailed team development, skills development workshops and leadership coaching.

There was one employee who was always gossiping, stirring the pot and

CHAPTER 8: *creating a safe environment*

> *giving the leader a really hard time. However, by the end of the programme when someone said something negative about the leader she responded by saying: "Do you have any idea how much she backs us up? She takes so much flack so we can have the freedoms we have as a team, so instead of judging her why don't you try and stand in her shoes."*
>
> *I was gob-smacked when I heard this comment from the very person who used to cause drama. I did an invisible air punch that day. But to get to this point, everyone has to be willing to learn, let go and move to a space of vulnerability.*

How to create a safe space

As a leader, it's crucial for you to consider what environment you are creating for your team.

→ How do you react to and deal with your team members mistakes?
→ What do you do when you make a mistake?
→ What example are you setting?
→ Are you able to admit your mistakes and share them with the team?
→ Do you show vulnerability when you don't have the answer or when you are worried?

If you don't demonstrate positive behaviour yourself why on earth would your team members believe you when you say: "mistakes are an opportunity to learn". Why should they admit their mistakes and share their learnings when you don't share yours?

Think about the life positions discussed in chapter five. Are you dealing with people in a respectful manner or are you operating from *I'm okay, You're not okay*, where you make people feel small? If you learn to operate from *I'm okay, You're okay* where people feel valued, you will set your team up for high engagement, productivity and performance.

1. Start by setting aside some time to consider your interactions over the last week. Did you do anything that could have caused people to be in the anxiety zone? Are you offering your team members too little support? Are you challenging someone too much? Is there anyone that you nurture too much thereby disempowering them from taking ownership? Reflect to see if there are any patterns that emerge with specific people.

2. Then schedule meetings with individuals in your team. It's best to start with people that you are very comfortable with. Set the scene for the chat by saying that the

session is for you to develop and grow as the leader. Ask for brutal honesty – even if it's going to be hard to hear. Take notes of your feedback.

Ask your team members the following questions:
→ *How often do you avoid asking questions because you are concerned about my reaction?*
→ *Do you think I admit my mistakes when I make them?*
→ *Was there ever a time when you were not comfortable admitting your mistakes?*
→ *In which scenarios do you find it hard to challenge me on my thinking process?*
→ *How often do you have ideas that you don't share?*
→ *What is the reason for not sharing these ideas?*
→ *What can I do to make you feel more comfortable to ask questions, admit mistakes, offer ideas or challenge the status quo?*
→ *How would you like me to challenge you more?*
It may be difficult to hear some truths about yourself but it's important to be vulnerable.

3 Once you have chatted with your team members, I suggest that you get them together and share what you have learnt about yourself as a leader. It's always a good idea to show your human side and admit your shortcomings.

4 Then discuss what actions you are going to implement based on their feedback. Thank your team for their honest feedback and mention that you will focus on developing a feedback culture across the team.

Chapter checklist

☐ Reflect on what kind of environment you are fostering for your team.
☐ Discuss the safety model. Identify which safety state your team is in.
☐ Schedule one-on-one meetings with team members. Ask them questions about the team environment and the impact you have as a leader.
☐ Consider what you have learnt and devise a list of steps to make the team environment a more psychologically safe place.

chapter 9

Building trust

We've all heard the expression "trust is earned not given". This is especially true in the business world where trust is like your stock. The higher your trustworthiness, the better your value is on the stock exchange. People are only willing to work with you or buy your product or service if they have faith in you. Without trust your business will mean nothing. You could spearhead team talks, create engagement and inspiration but without trust your team members will say what you want to hear and say something different behind your back. Remember that if your team members, customers or superiors don't trust you, you aren't squat. *Nothing but a job title.*

The question is: how can you inspire trust? Charles Green, author of *The Trusted Advisor*, developed the trust equation comprising four variables to measure a person's trustworthiness.

$$\text{TRUST} = \frac{\text{Credibilty} + \text{Reliability} + \text{Intimacy}}{\text{Self-interest}}$$

According to this equation, credibility, reliability and intimacy increase your trustworthiness, while a high level of self-interest can decrease it. When all four components are in balance, a person will begin to trust you. By understanding this equation, you can pinpoint which areas you excel in and which areas may require some work. Let's explore this equation...

CREDIBILITY

what you say

As Green explains, establishing credibility is all about your words. It's important that people can trust that what you say is the truth. Therefore, it's important to be accurate and logical. To be an expert you need to be well informed and versed in your field of interest. Establishing yourself as an expert in your field means knowing the facts, trends and latest developments. People are not fools. You can tell when someone doesn't know what they're talking about. Limited knowledge hinders credibility. So if you're looking to increase your credibility, do your homework and increase your expertise or skillset.

> I'm going to use one of our clients in the pressure instrumentation industry as an example. We worked with about 15 members of their sales team. We spearheaded a workshop that focused on the trust equation and many of them realised that while they sell radar instruments and they knew their product well, they weren't staying abreast of what was happening in the industry. So to set themselves apart from the competition, they needed to know the industry inside out. Meanwhile the newbies in the team were very frustrated because they hadn't built relationships with their clients. They realised that they needed to do a deep dive into product training to increase their knowledge and show that they knew their stuff. Think about it, if you lack credibility people will think you are flaky or pretending to know something. *And we know how that goes down.*

Think about this:
→ As a leader how credible are you?
→ Does your team have credibility in the business and with other stakeholders?
→ Do you and your team know your stuff?

RELIABILITY   *what you do*

This all comes down to your actions. If you tell someone you are going to do something and you don't do it, then you will lose their trust. This is incredibly important for me. As a business leader, it's crucial that team members deliver on their promises and I can trust them to take care of things even when I'm not around. And it goes vice versa. When I promise to do something, I need to deliver by the deadline.

Reliability also comes down to how much you engage with someone. The more you interact, the more opportunities you will have to see if you can rely on an individual. When someone consistently behaves the same way, it's seen as a repeated experience and you come to understand what you can expect from him or her. This is why we trust people that we know well or work with often.

You can increase your reliability by delivering on your word. Without reliability you will be seen as irresponsible. There are two options in this regard. You can either increase your delivery or adjust your commitment and only agree to things you can actually deliver on. Always do what you say you are going to do. It's the most effective way to build trust and reliability.

CHAPTER 9: *building trust*

> I remember when we were dealing with a start-up in the fitness and data aggregation industry. They landed their first listed client. In the beginning the client's Procurement Manager was extremely hard and tough. I remember the Managing Director saying: "Damn she is a tough cookie. I don't know how to get her to trust us."
>
> Now three years later they have an extremely strong, transparent and effective professional relationship. Why? Her repeated experience of exceptional service, problem solving and trouble shooting. Every interaction was always consistent. The strategy worked. Don't over promise, be transparent around costs and always deliver on time. *It's not that difficult. Just plan better, show up and do what you are supposed to do.*

Think about this:
→ As a leader, do you follow through on what you promise? *We often forget that our colleagues are our clients*
→ How reliable is your team with different stakeholders and external and internal clients?
→ Do you engage enough with your team so they experience repeated consistent behaviour from you? And make damn sure that your actions are positive!

INTIMACY

Some of you might roll your eyes at the thought of sharing your emotions in the workplace, but intimacy is not about divulging your deepest secrets or expressing every emotion. It's about connecting on a human level. If you are an Analyser or Driver, you will have to learn what works well for you because without intimacy you will struggle with trust. *Yes, I'm stereotyping here but the majority of us need to hear this.*

Building intimacy with your team members, clients, peers or your executive team requires you to open up about who you are. It entails being vulnerable and sharing details of your personal life, as well as your thoughts, feelings, doubts or even fears. If you're the one that is trying to build trust, guess what, you need to be able to take a risk so that the other person can see that you are willing to open up. That's how intimacy starts flourishing. And don't expect the other person to immediately go there, they need to learn that they can trust you first.

I often share very intimate details with my clients but I do it at a time when I feel comfortable. It's like selective transparency. My client relationships are very strong because we know a lot about each other and we have developed emotional closeness. If you know someone on a personal level you are more likely to stick your neck out for them. To know is to trust. By expressing vulnerability about who you are, you are building intimacy, which in turn builds trust. Find what works for you, but don't fall into a comfort zone and only make small talk about the weather or the traffic – that is not intimacy people!

I know what you're thinking. Men don't show their emotions.
Back to the radar instruments sales team. The team was mostly made up of men who were age 35+. The team's clients were mostly men too but that didn't mean that intimacy wasn't important. So we encouraged team members to start sharing stories about their work experience, their children, hunting trips, fears about getting older and concerns about the industry. We also listed questions that they could ask their clients:
→ I heard that things are changing in your industry, do you have any concerns?
→ I see you have a picture of your son on your desk, how old is he?
→ How was your fishing trip last weekend?
And when someone asks how you are, instead of giving a generic response, actually answer the questions and say: "I'm well, thanks. I must admit, I have had better days, but I'm happy to be here."

Think about this:
→ As a leader how much vulnerability do you show? How often do you share your thoughts or feelings?
→ How do your team members connect with each other and with clients? Do they just get to the point or do they make an effort to really connect?
→ Do you have the guts to show your team how to increase intimacy? If you don't do it, how can you expect them to?

SELF-INTEREST

Is your focus on your own personal gain?
Self-obsession is a terrible trait.

This all boils down to your agenda. How much do you align with the interest of others? Is your attention and focus on succeeding or winning or are you genuinely concerned with doing what is best for your clients or team members? Highly self-orientated people are hard to trust because they are more interested in themselves than the people they are working with.

If someone suspects that you are only concerned about what's in it for you, they are less likely to trust you. Think about yourself as a leader, is your main focus on your goals or is your self-interest at a healthy level where people can see that you are in it for the benefit of everyone.

I'm not saying that you shouldn't think about your own goals and desires. There needs

CHAPTER 9: *building trust*

to be some value for you, but you should never put your needs ahead of others. I find that a self interest level of 3/10 works well for me. From my own experience if I detect that someone's self interest is higher than that, I immediately start thinking about how I can duck out of the conversation or engagement.

> *Coming back to the sales team… They were so concerned about their sales target that it became an obsession and they neglected to pay attention to the needs of their clients. Thankfully this changed when they realised that commission is not the goal. Having an incredible happy and satisfied client that you trust and have a long-term relationship with – now that's the goal.*
>
> *Very recently this company went as far as removing all sales targets and focusing on the needs of the client. Their goal is to serve, engage and build strong relationships. I'm not saying that you should remove targets all together, I can assure you I have them too. But as a leader, it's your responsibility to show your clients and team members that you aren't just there to get ahead. You need to show them that you are truly interested and not simply milking them for your own benefit.*

Think about this:
→ As a leader, what do you care about? Is your focus mostly on your career path or do you actually have your team's back?
→ What kind of work environment are you creating? Do you give team members the space to be interested in each other?

The trust equation is connected to psychological safety. If you can create an environment where your team members are in the learning zone with healthy levels of safety and accountability, people will trust you and they will want to follow you. If you have the trust of your team members and you challenge them or put them in a position where they may feel uncomfortable, they will be willing because they know that you will offer them support. So, what does it look like when one of the four trust components are lacking?
→ If **credibility** is lacking, you will appear as flaky.
→ When **reliability** is lacking, you will be seen as irresponsible.
→ If there is little **intimacy**, you may seem cold or distant.
→ When your **self-interest** is too high, you will be regarded as devious.

Now that you understand the recipe for trust, you need to consider what you are doing as a team leader to be seen as trustworthy. Consider how much your team trusts you, as well as how much you trust your team. Lastly, how much trust do your clients or partners have in your team?

It's important to foster an environment of trust within your team. Arrange a meeting and ask your team members if they trust one another. Explore and discuss. A workshop that focuses on trust is where the most amazing conversations start, but you need to plan and facilitate this well. Then determine how much trust your clients have in your team. You could do a survey or engage with someone in the client sphere that could share insights.

As a team, discuss the following:
→ How can we be seen as more credible? How can we show that we know what we're talking about and that we've done our homework?
→ What do we need to implement to be seen as more reliable? How can we show that we deliver on our promises?
→ Share ideas on how to improve intimacy. Some people are naturally good at connecting with people on an emotional level, while others struggle. What can we learn from each other? How can team members develop a sense of closeness with each other and with clients?
→ Do we have a healthy level of self-interest? If not, what can we do to address it?

Chapter checklist

☐ As a team leader, consider how much trust your team members, clients and management have in you.
☐ Familiarise yourself with the trust equation. Reflect on how much credibility, reliability, intimacy and self-interest you demonstrate in your role.
☐ Determine where you are lacking and develop a plan to improve on your shortcomings.
☐ Meet with your team members and discuss how much trust exists within the team and with clients.
☐ Discuss what the team can do to improve credibility, reliability and intimacy and develop a healthy sense of self-interest. 💬

chapter 10

Effective listening skills

Many leaders love the sound of their own voice. They tend to talk too much without taking the time to actively listen and understand what their team members have to say. Not listening results in a work environment that isn't operating at its optimum.

Listening is a skill that many people lack. When you have deadlines to meet, meetings to attend and multiple projects to juggle, it's easy to be distracted. Also, when you listen to someone talk it's tempting to think about what you are going to say in response, so you neglect to actually hear what the speaker is saying. Several studies have found that the most common cause of conflict is misunderstanding. *Which can be prevented if you just slow down, shut up and listen!*

Taking the time to understand another person's viewpoint lays the foundation for mutual understanding and a clear exchange of information. When a team member feels heard, it makes a huge difference to their motivation, engagement and productivity.

> *I remember an instance when I was working with a financial services team and one of the team members drew a picture of the Financial Director, but in the image he had two mouths and one ear. The Financial Director was laughing because he thought it was funny. But leaders, this is not something to be proud about. This is a real problem!*

I came across three different levels of listening when I did my transactional analysis training in 2009. However, no one is certain who came up with this listening model, so please excuse the fact that I don't have a reference here.

The three levels of listening are extremely useful for all leaders:

| 1 **internal listening** | The voice in your head. | 2 **paraphrasing** | Saying it in your own words, back to the person. | 3 **deeper listening** | Listen beyond what you hear. |

1. Internal listening

This is described as shallow listening because the focus is on yourself and your own thoughts rather than the speaker. You are concerned with your own opinions, judgments, feelings and conclusions. Internal listening is suitable for situations such as looking at a menu or asking for directions, but it does not bode well for connecting with people or coaching a team member.

This is often when assumptions are made.

The problem is that there is a tendency to listen to the voices in your head without really hearing or understanding the speaker. This voice can be positive, but it can also be judgmental and damaging. This is when communication fails because you hear what's in your head as opposed to what the person is actually saying.

> I have a coaching client, who admits that he cannot listen past this point and what often happens is that he immediately creates a non-safe space because team members observe his facial expressions and they can tell that he is thinking negative thoughts such as:
> → You are just complaining and your point is not valid.
> → You are talking utter rubbish.
> → What on earth are you saying? You don't know the facts.

All these inner thoughts prevent you from listening well. So often we jump to conclusions without knowing all the facts. If this team leader put a bit more effort into understanding why his team members are experiencing issues or what the complaint is, he might find that the speaker is there to brainstorm solutions rather than complain. However, due to his poor listening skills he breaks down the channels of communication.

Always consider what your inner voice is saying. Are you being negative or judgmental? If so, think about why you are reacting that way. When you listen to someone, always come from a place of *I'm okay, You're okay.* If you want to add to the conversation, try saying: "What I'm thinking after hearing what you have to say is...." This phrase is useful to create a very safe and transparent relationship and it helps to clear the air from the beginning.

> I contacted my senior facilitator this week to check if she was interested in a project. She responded with a series of questions (which were sent via WhatsApp) and my immediate gut feel was: "What is with her attitude? Damn, it seems like she is only interested in money and easy projects." My inner voice was very strong and I got annoyed. We have the kind of relationship where I can voice my thoughts. So I sent her a voice note.

In retrospect, I should have picked up the phone and called – but it worked out thankfully.

CHAPTER 10: *effective listening skills*

> The voice note said: "I just want to check in with you because my assumptions are running wild. Before it turns into a conviction, I want to check if everything is okay because I am sensing some resistance. It seems as though you are more concerned about money than you are about the impact of this project."
>
> She immediately responded: "Thanks for checking in and that's not the case at all. I'm just working through everything that is on my plate and I'm busy with financial planning, so I feel slightly overwhelmed. I'm totally onboard and excited."
>
> Had I acted on my inner voice and treated it as fact, I would have broken a lot of trust between the two of us and potentially created unnecessary drama. This is why it's so important to be wary of the voices and assumptions in your head.

2 Paraphrasing

The next level of listening focuses on the other person. This is when you listen more deeply to what they are saying and you are truly present. At this stage, you should repeat what the person has said in your own words. This allows you to check that you have understood them and it gives the speaker an opportunity to reflect and process. It's amazing how much processing happens when someone paraphrases what you have said. I often hear responses such as:

→ "Yes, that's exactly what I mean."
→ "Now that I hear you say it, I realise it's not such a big deal and it sounds silly."
→ "No, that's not what I mean. Let me explain it differently."

All these responses are great and it shows that it gave the speaker the opportunity to process their own thoughts and as the listener, you get to check your understanding.

As discussed in chapter 6, this is particularly effective when conducting a coaching session. The most effective way to coach is to listen, reflect, ask questions and repeat.

Karen Pratt's art of listening graph

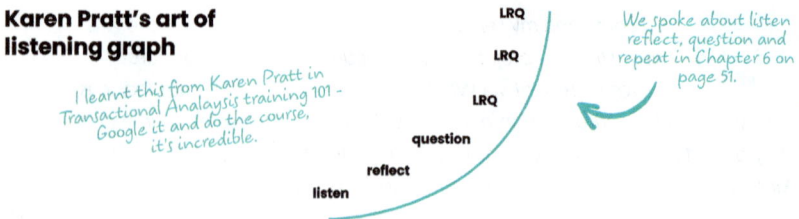

I learnt this from Karen Pratt in Transactional Analaysis training 101 - Google it and do the course, it's incredible.

We spoke about listen reflect, question and repeat in Chapter 6 on page 51.

It creates a platform for reflection and processing and shows the person that you are listening on a deeper level.

For this type of listening to be effective, it's crucial that you give 100% of your focus. Close your laptop, put away your phone and turn your body towards the person you are listening to. It's great to have a go-to line when doing this so you can get used to it. The phrases that I use include:

→ "So what I hear you saying is…"
→ "So just for my own understanding, you are saying…"
→ "I want to clarify what you said…"

For example, if a team member says they feel overwhelmed and explains that they are experiencing last minute deadline pressure. You could respond by saying: "What I hear you saying is that you feel frustrated when I give you last minute deadlines because you're already so overwhelmed."

This gives the team member the opportunity to share and process. Then they could respond by saying: "Exactly. I would prefer it if you could give me enough time to tackle new tasks."

3 Deeper listening

This entails focusing on the speaker's energy. It involves using all your senses to read between the lines and observe non-verbal cues such as body language or tone of voice. This requires you to tap into your own assumptions, values or background. It's about listening to what the speaker has not explicitly said.

Deeper listening requires awareness, so if you don't pay full attention and tend to look at your phone, check your emails or focus on the people around you in the coffee shop – learning to listen properly will be very, very hard for you.

My pet peeve is when I'm talking to someone and I can see they are eyeing their phone or checking messages coming through.

I lose respect for people who do this.

If this is how you behave with your team members, friends or family members, rather tell them you aren't in right space or frame of mind to listen to what they want to talk about. You're doing more damage by pretending to listen than being honest and telling them that you don't have capacity for that type of conversation. I can go on about this for hours, but I will stop here.

CHAPTER 10: *effective listening skills*

When you are listening, it's important to consider the person's situation and frame of mind. You could say:

> → "What comes up for me when I hear you say that is…"
> → "Wow! I have to share what I was thinking while you were saying…"
> → "I might be totally wrong, but I think it's worth sharing what's on my mind…"
> → "I have a question related to what you said…"

For example, you could say to your team member: "I've noticed that you seem overwhelmed a lot lately and it seems as though your confidence has taken a knock."

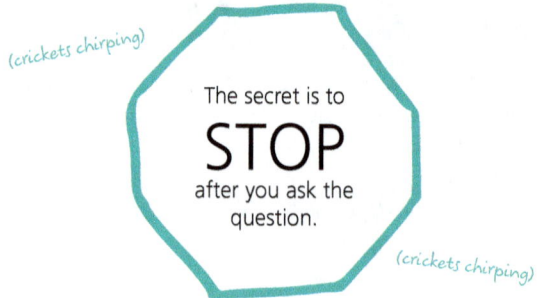

(crickets chirping)

The secret is to **STOP** after you ask the question.

(crickets chirping)

I have sat in on some of my client's meetings and so often the leader asks a brilliant question but instead of waiting for a response, he or she keeps talking. Make sure you give the team member the opportunity to answer the question.

The team member may respond by saying. "That's true. This new project requires me to tap into a new skill set and I'm finding some tasks super challenging. I think I'd perform better and build my confidence if you could give me more time to work on things."

And PLEASE be aware of when to keep your mouth shut.

This conversation could have gone badly if you relied on your inner voice and judged the person for being lazy or incompetent. But by practicing deeper listening you are able to foster mutual understanding and increase trust and engagement.

→ To become a better listener, you need to be aware. When you are listening to someone speak, be mindful of which level of listening you are practicing.

→ If you find yourself getting stuck at level one, write down your assumptions and question them. Consider why you are going to a judgmental or negative space and consider what you can do to prevent it from happening in the future.

→ Try writing things down so that you don't have to remember them. Take note of your first thoughts and then dig a bit deeper.

→ After you reflect on your own listening habits, think about how your team members listen to you, as well as clients and peers. If there is a lack of listening skills in the team, spearhead a short workshop and ask the team to rate their ability to listen. Explain the three levels of listening and discuss. Then ask your team members to draw up a list of ways to improve.

Fostering a culture of listening will help everyone feel safe and psychologically supported. Listening well can result in more trust and engagement, which translates to better performance.

I worked with an executive team in the tourism industry, who constantly interrupted each other during meetings. Of course, this is one of the easiest ways to build frustration. It felt a bit like a school instruction, but we made a new rule that worked so well. The new rule was:
→ *You are NOT allowed to interrupt, under any circumstances. You can only start speaking once the person has stopped.*
→ *The speaker must respect their airtime and get to the point quickly.*
→ *My favourite: If you have a question, you need to ask it before you are allowed to comment or give your opinion.*

These very simple steps changed the whole flow of the team's meetings. People felt heard because they had the time to ask and respond to questions and get their message across.

Chapter checklist

- ☐ Familiarise yourself with the three levels of listening.
- ☐ Analyse your own listening habits. Which level of listening is your go to?
- ☐ Determine what steps you can take to improve your listening.
- ☐ Tell a team member that you are trying to improve and explain what the steps are and ask them to give you feedback after team meetings.
- ☐ Question how well your team listens to you.
- ☐ If necessary meet with your team to discuss the different levels and offer tips for them to improve.

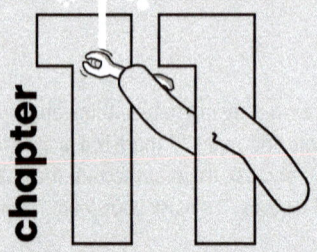

chapter 11

Fostering a proactive team
And taking ownership

Lately, it seems like there is always something to worry about, whether it's the economy, politics, or the health and safety of our loved ones. And while it's easy to say "don't sweat the small stuff", it isn't as easy to put into practice. Let's be honest. Sometimes life can just suck.

Everyone has stuff they worry about. The little monsters in your head that keep you out of sleep and drain your energy. News flash: You can take back control and do something about it! It all comes down to being proactive. Part of a high performance team is having team members that are accountable and take responsibility. Your team members need to think proactively instead of waiting for things to happen. *If you haven't gotten it yet, you need to change your mindset to one of proactiveness and ownership.*

The model for this chapter comes from one of my favourite books, *The 7 Habits of Highly Effective People* by Stephen R. Covey. This chapter will help you to view the situations you find yourself in differently and tackle them with the mindset of "what can I do to make this work for me". You will be able to hold yourself accountable as a leader and proactively guide your team to do the same.

As you work through the model, do your own reflection first to measure your performance with regards to responsibility and proactiveness. Then discuss it with your team to see how proactive they are and how they can improve.

THE CIRCLE OF CONCERN

Covey explains that each person has a number of things or situations that concern them. Imagine collecting all of these concerns into one big circle and calling it the Circle of Concern.

When I discuss this concept with various teams, there are similar concerns that come up time and time again. At work, many people worry about their boss or difficult colleagues, performance reviews, business travel, clients and deadlines. On a personal level, worries include finances, politics, crime, in-laws or the health of their family. Each person has their own list of concerns. Take two minutes to draw a big circle and write these concerns inside the circle but close to the edge. *Do it now before you continue reading.*

Stephen R. Covey's Proactive focus model

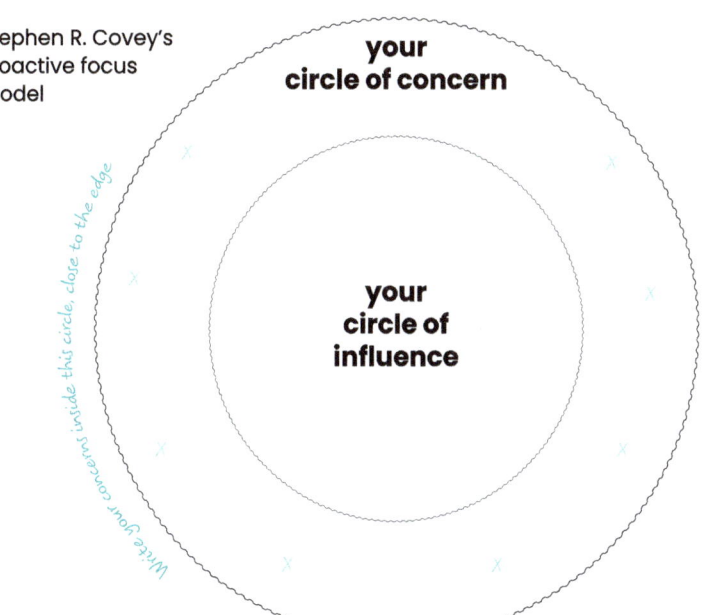

your circle of concern

your circle of influence

Write your concerns inside this circle, close to the edge

While it's perfectly normal to be concerned about these things, what's important is how you react to them. If you don't do anything to address or change your situation, these worries will simply stay in your Circle of Concern, drain your energy and negatively affect your state of mind. And this will rob you of your time.

The problem with this circle is that many of the things that we are concerned about are outside of our control, or at least we think and believe we can't do anything about it – things like inflation, your manager's personality or retrenchments. It's normal to feel like your hands are tied and there is nothing you can do.

> We recently lost a big retainer client due to impact of COVID-19 and I remember saying to my husband as I burst into tears from exhaustion and stress: "Babes, my forecast is screwed!" *I used a stronger word.*
> His response to me was: "Seriously, what you say is what you attract into the world. *Yes, yes, but this is different, I thought.*
> Then he challenged me: "So how are you going to deal with this so you aren't so screwed? Stop feeling sorry for yourself because screwed is the last thing you are."
> This is a typical example of how easy it is to spend time in your Circle of Concern. Proactive people, however, are aware that they are "response-able" which means that even though they may not be able to change the situation, they know that they have control over how they respond. They focus their time and energy on the things that they can influence, instead of wasting time on the things they can't.

THE CIRCLE OF INFLUENCE

This circle is made up of the things that you can do something about. It all boils down to determining what you can do to make your situation better. You can tailor your actions and use your energy to build an environment where you are addressing and working on the things that concern you. Moving concerns from your Circle of Concern to your Circle of Influence requires a lot of work or a change of mindset.

The first step is to look at your concerns and divide them into three categories:

1 Direct control

These concerns are directly within your control because they are related to your own habits and behaviours. For example, one of your concerns could be the state of your health. Perhaps you aren't getting enough rest or you feel burnt out a lot of the time. This is in your direct control because there are steps that you can take to address the issue. You could establish a proper sleep routine by switching off all screens an hour before bedtime and going to bed at reasonable hour every night. You could improve your diet or take a multivitamin to better fuel your body.

If you are concerned about one of your team member's skillset, you have direct control to put processes in place to develop the team member. You could assign a training buddy or create an on-the-job learning programme. While you might not have direct control over how much they learn, there are things you can do to address your concerns. My guess is that many leaders just complain about what shitty employees they have, without taking a real interest in what they can do to increase their skillset. It's easy to absolve yourself of responsibility and we do it more often than we think. Don't get me wrong, there are amazing leaders out there but I'm talking to the ones who expect their team members to perform but don't provide the platform for them to do so.

2 Indirect control

Issues that involve other people are in your indirect control. You cannot control the behaviour or actions of others but you can work on how you react to them. For example, you may not be able to influence how your board or management behave, but you can control how you respond. You can control the quality of your work by figuring out what concerns or triggers the board and producing work that speaks to what they want. Furthermore, when your peers or superiors are in a bad mood, you can choose not to allow it to affect you. Are you going to respond from your Parent or Child ego states or are you going to step up and be an actual adult (chapter 3)?

3 No control

There are some issues that you may not have any direct or indirect control over such as the economy or politics of your country, but you can choose to respond with hope or despair. How you react to our environment is totally within your control. You have the power to let it go and not waste your energy on it.

I want to challenge you here. Even though you might not have any control over the politics of the country and thus technically shouldn't waste time on it, it's easier said than done. So what you can do is focus your efforts on understanding the policies of the different political parties. You could take the time to investigate what they stand for, what you like and don't like, agree with and don't agree with. Instead of wasting energy on worrying about it, you can try to understand it better by investigating and speaking to people who are in the know, so that you can make informed decisions. Just imagine what type of team you would have if everyone or a few team members had this attitude and mindset?

It's important to focus on the concerns that you can influence. The more you focus on your Circle of Influence, the bigger it will become. And let's be real, if I see someone taking control or embodying this attitude, I admire and respect them.

In my experience, what stops so many individuals and teams from expanding their Circle of Influence is when they are presented with potential solutions but they respond with: "yes, but". I don't have patience for this. By all means feel free to complain, but only if you make a decision about what you are going to do about your problem. If you aren't going to take action to improve your situation then you don't get to complain. It's so important that as a leader, you need to model behaviour where you don't just talk about what is bothering you. You take action to fix it.

When you focus on growing your Circle of Influence, you begin to realise that you are capable of controlling your circumstances. Your confidence will grow because you will feel more in control each time you take ownership of your environment. You will also be seen as more credible, accountable and proactive.

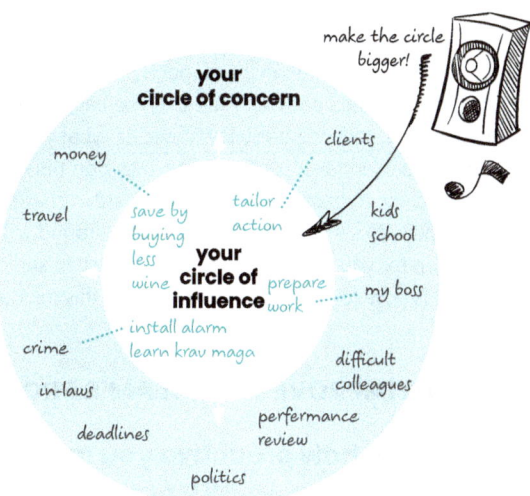

CHAPTER 11: *fostering a proactive team*

There are two factors that negatively impact a person's ability to be proactive:

1 Justification
This is when a person finds reasons or excuses for why they aren't able to do something or change their environment. For example, a team member who says they are too old or too young for a promotion. They are simply limiting themselves and giving away their power.

2 Laying blame
This happens when you blame someone else for the fact that you didn't do something. For example, a team member who claims that they were unable to meet their deadline because they were waiting on a report from a colleague. The important question is: did they follow up with their colleague or simply wait around?

RESPONSIBILITY

Responsibility is the ability to choose your response to a situation and environment.

Think about how often you lay blame or justify your actions. We are all guilty of it, and it is so counterproductive. Instead you should always take responsibility. So many people are afraid of this word. Many think that if you take responsibility you are taking the blame or you're saying you are at fault. This is not entirely true. True individual power lies in the ability to choose how you respond to a situation. It's about stepping up and doing what's in your control to better your situation.

Think about what you would do.

In his book, *The Subtle Art of Not Giving a F*ck,* Mark Manson tells a story: Your doorbell rings and when you open the door there is a baby left on your doorstep. Abandoned. It's not your fault that the baby is there. You didn't make this happen. However, it's your responsibility to decide what you are going to do with that baby.

When a person takes responsibility, they don't blame the outside world. They don't wait for things to happen for them. They are in charge and they work on their Circle of Influence. When you do this, the people around you will have greater respect and admiration for you. You will be seen as proactive and as someone who takes ownership. Your job is now to guide your team to have this mindset.

HOW TO IMPROVE YOUR TEAM'S PROACTIVENESS

1 Consider how proactive you are
Do you stew over your concerns or are you proactive in taking steps to address the issues you are concerned about? What kind of behaviour are you demonstrating to your team?

Draw up your Circle of Concern and your Circle of Influence. Where are you currently spending most of your time? Worrying or doing something about it? What are you currently doing to change your circumstances? Which concerns would you like to move into the Circle of Influence? Consider what changes you need to implement to do so.

2 Discuss with your team

In a workshop, ask your team members to reflect on how proactive they are. Do a quick overview of the Circles of Concern and Influence. Ask them to identify where they spend their time and what they can we do to increase their Circle of Influence. Ask each person to identify an activity that they can do to take control of each area of concern. Together, you can become more proactive.

> *One of the software development teams I work with utilised this model. Together the team completed a Circle of Concern and talked it over. Once they were done, they separated into smaller groups and brainstormed solutions for each concern in the circle. Each group came up with a list of action steps to address small but important issues. Then the team came back together to discuss the best way forward. The leader didn't have to do anything because the team members came up with all the solutions. #winning*

Chapter checklist

- ☐ Consider how proactive you are. How are you showing up for your team?
- ☐ Complete your Circle of Concern. What does it look like?
- ☐ Now create your Circle of Influence. What can you do to make your Circle of Concern smaller? Compile a list of action steps to address your concerns.
- ☐ Arrange a workshop with your team. Explain the Circles of Concern and Influence. Ask each person to identify where they spend their time, and what they can do to increase their Circle of Influence.

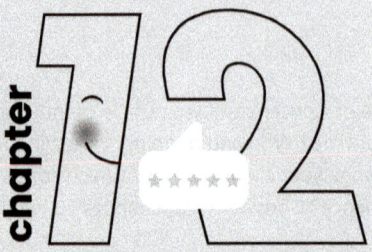

How to give amazing feedback

Feedback is essential in any company. Full stop. When done right, it can take your team from average to high performance because it promotes personal growth. And it's probably my favourite thing to do with teams because the energy you receive while doing it and the value people get from it is just incredible.

Fostering a feedback culture within your team can also boost productivity, help everyone stay on track and enable team members to overcome and learn from their mistakes. Please don't kid yourself into believing that because you do monthly one-on-ones or annual performance reviews that your team has a feedback culture.

You are just fooling yourself.

While positive feedback leaves people feeling appreciated and upbeat, giving negative feedback is not so easy. If it's not done in a respectful and non-judgmental manner, it can hurt people, lower their self-esteem and make them feel underappreciated. So it's crucial that you watch your mouth and plan what you are going to say. You have the ability to either screw it up or grow an incredibly strong team that is able to smash their goals.

This is the last chapter but like the others, it doesn't stand on its own. All of the skills and techniques you learnt about in previous chapters need to come into play.

The Johari Window Model

Before we jump into tips for giving and receiving feedback, I'd like to look at a psychological tool that was created by Joseph Luft and Harry Ingham in 1955, that allows individuals to enhance their self-awareness. It's based on the idea that in a group, trust can be acquired through sharing information about yourself and learning from other people's feedback. The model consists of four quadrants:

This makes me think about the trust equation in chapter 9.

1 Open self

Any information or thoughts that you are aware of and have shared with others forms part of your Open Self. This includes your behaviour, emotions, feelings, skills and views. Building trust with others requires you to disclose information about yourself and learn about others based on what they share with you.

For example, when you join a new team, you reveal personal information about yourself such as your background and experience. The more information you share, the larger this quadrant becomes.

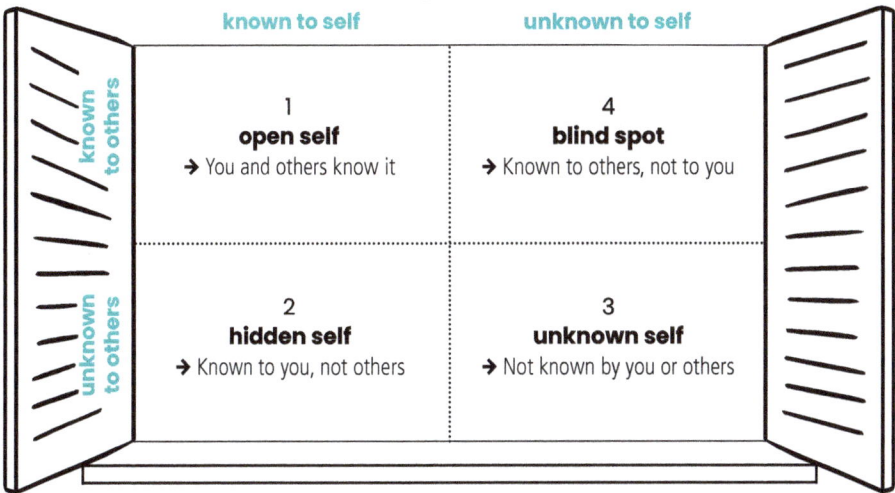

2. Hidden self

This consists of the information or parts of yourself that you keep hidden from others. This could include your feelings, past experiences, fears and secrets. We have a tendency to keep some things hidden if we feel that it's irrelevant or private, or we fear being judged.

For example, I get very anxious when I talk to a board of executives. The board members don't know that I am nervous or stressed because I keep it to myself. If I inform them about my state of mind, that information moves from Hidden Self to Open Self.

3. Unknown self

This quadrant refers to the information that is unknown to you and others. This includes facts, feelings and talents that you are unaware of because you have not yet discovered them. For example, you may be really gifted at coaching or public speaking but you have not had the opportunity to try it so your abilities are undiscovered.

4. Blind spot

Your Blind Spot or Blind Self refers to what other people know or have observed about you, but you are unaware of. This can be a bitter pill to swallow because others may perceive you or your actions differently than you expect. For example, your team members might see you as aloof, while you think of yourself as warm.

The good thing about your Blind Spot is that feedback from others allows you to become aware of some of your positive and negative traits as perceived by others.

CHAPTER 12: *how to give amazing feedback*

Armed with this information, you can do self-reflection and development to address the negative aspects of your personality.

As a leader, it's advisable to ask your team members or colleagues for feedback on your abilities as a leader. When you are on the receiving end of feedback, be open to what people say. Don't justify or defend yourself, rather listen to the feedback, take it in, reflect on it and see what you can learn from it. Then figure out ways to improve your negative blind spot qualities.

Some people become addicted to finding out what their blind spots are because it presents opportunities for growth. When people give you feedback and you work on your blind spots it increases the Open Self quadrant and this area will become bigger. And that's the goal: to increase the open self. That's why feedback is so effective.

How to effectively give feedback

Some leaders cringe at the thought of criticising their team members, while others revel at the chance to tell someone off. Remember that negative feedback is hard to give and receive and there may be some raw emotions involved so try to show some understanding.

Feedback shouldn't only occur once a year in the form of a performance review. It should be fluid and take place regularly. Furthermore, it needn't be an awkward conversation with lots of fidgeting and a lack of eye contact. Feedback is most effective when it's to the point and done respectfully in a safe place.

Giving constructive feedback is a delicate balance that can be accomplished by implementing the D4 Model, which was created by Insights Discovery. The model is structured to accommodate the four personality types and will be effective whether the person is driven by data, emotions or action.

Please note there are many feedback models that are incredible. I have chosen this one because it taps into what we learnt about different personality types in chapter 2.

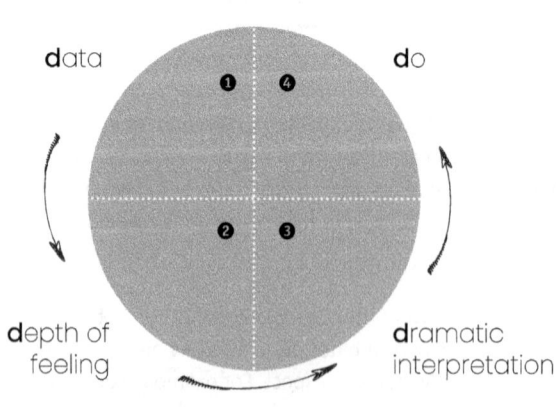

Insight Discovery's
D4 feedback model

You've seen this model before, on page 35

86

1. Data *Speaks to the Analyser (page 14)*

You should always start with the facts. Discuss what actually happened and where possible, use real and relevant examples so the person knows exactly what situation you are referring to. Examples offer context and ensure that you are both on the same page.

Some useful ways to introduce the topic include:
→ "When _____ happened..."
→ "When you did _____..."
→ "The report that you handed over to me yesterday was...."

For example:
"When you agreed to complete the document two weeks ago, I thought it would be taken care of. In today's meeting, however, you asked to revisit this deadline because you have not started working on it yet."

2. Depth of feeling *Speaks to the Amiable (page 15)*

The next step is to explain how you feel about the situation. Perhaps it was something you observed or something that was done to you. Explaining what you are going through helps the person to see things from your perspective.

Voice your feelings but don't blow it out of proportion. Use statements with the word "I" such as "I felt angry" or "I'm hurt" as opposed to attacking statements such as: "you did" or "you made me angry". Also avoid using words such as "always" or "never".

Try one of these sentences:
→ "When that happened I felt ..."
→ "I must admit that hurt me because...."
→ "I'm getting frustrated because..."

For example:
"This caused a lot of frustration for me and I must admit I'm getting angry because this isn't the first time this has happened."

87

CHAPTER 12: *how to give amazing feedback*

speaks to the Expressive (page 16)

3 Dramatic Interpretation

How are you interpreting the situation? What impact has it had? It's important to discuss your reflections about how the scenario has affected you, other team members or the company. This can reveal what stories <u>you are telling yourself</u>. *Remember when we discussed how to have tough conversations in chapter 4. Master your own stories.*

> **Explain the impact by saying:**
> → "What I see now…"
> → "What I learnt from this is…"
> → "The impact of your actions were…"
> → "I'm starting to wonder if…"

For example:
"I hope you understand how this impacts the workflow of the project and puts pressure on the team. It really feels as if you are disrupting this project on purpose."

4 Do   *speaks to the Driver (page 13)*

Focus on the action steps moving forward. Discuss what you want to do and what you'd like the other person to do.

> **Try one of these sentences:**
> → "This is what I suggest…"
> → "What I would do moving forward…"
> → "What I would love to see…"

For example:
"In the future, what I suggest is that you communicate when you think you won't be able to meet your deadline. Also, don't agree to do something if you are unable to. Let me know what you need from me because I cannot accept another delay like this."

As a leader, it's important to consider how you give and receive feedback. The biggest mistake many leaders make is rushing to get to the outcome and the next steps. So often we explain the situation and then go straight to action. We totally miss the opportunity to give and receive feedback by not discussing how you are feeling and the impact. When you practice giving feedback, use this four-step process. If you are nervous about giving feedback, you can always use some tips from chapter 4 *(page 30)* on tough conversations.

> One of my clients is in the short-term property rental industry and when we started working together, they were already performing fairly well. The team was in the norming phase and they wanted to increase the connection between team members because they had only been working together for 12 months and some people were fairly new.
>
> So we created feedback circles. Each person had to make sure that they spoke to absolutely everyone in the team and as facilitators we coordinated this to make sure it flowed smoothly. *Think speed dating.*
>
> The idea is to give on-the-spot feedback about what a colleague can do better and then the other person gets to speak, so that both team members have an opportunity to give and receive feedback. Then you swap until everyone has had a chance to speak to each other.
>
> You can change these questions or statements depending on what you feel will work with your team.

You could use leading questions such as:
→ "What I think you do really well is…"
→ "What I would love to see you do differently…"
→ "What I wish for the two of us moving forward…"

These three simple questions had an enormous impact when we did this with various teams. One of my clients still speaks about feedback circles and how team members refer to what they learnt.

It's absolutely crucial that as a leader you must also be able to receive feedback without trying to justify or defend yourself.

As a rule of thumb:
→ You can only ask clarifying questions when receiving feedback.
→ Consider the feedback and then decide what you want to do with it.
→ You can choose to take it on or not.

If you justify or defend yourself when you receive feedback all you

CHAPTER 12: *how to give amazing feedback*

are doing is telling the person who gave you feedback that it's not a safe space. Why on earth would they give you information or feedback in the future? It's the quickest way to show your team members that you aren't open to growing. It also hinders high performance because that can very easily become the culture in your team or business.

Yes, YOU set that tone.

To kick start this process, select team members that would most benefit from feedback and then utilise the D4 model or the team feedback session. After the feedback session, ask your team members to reflect on whether the feedback was delivered in a constructive and helpful way. Ask them what they took away from it and what they would like to focus on.

To foster a feedback culture between team members, arrange a meeting to discuss. Ask each person to rate their ability to give and receive feedback. Explain the Johari Window Model and ask team members to analyse and discuss their blind spots and ways to reduce them. Then outline the D4 feedback model and encourage team members to implement it in their day-to-day interactions.

Check your blind spots!

Chapter checklist

- [ ] As a leader consider how effectively you give and receive feedback in your role.
- [ ] Analyse the Johari Window Model.
- [ ] Identify your blind spots by asking your colleagues, friends or family for feedback. Work on ways to tackle them.
- [ ] Choose team members who would benefit from feedback. Utilise the D4 model to give feedback.
- [ ] Discuss the model with the team and urge them to adopt it.

I hope you found value in this book. My hope is that you apply what you've learnt and achieve incredible performance with your team. Remember to visit our resources page for more great tools: http://bit.ly/guidingaction

Acknowledgments

I realised very early on that I'm a fan of high performance. It became evident during my netball career at school, when I was a student and in my professional career.
I've made significant career and business changes over the years because I strived towards having a high performance team where everyone is aligned and in sync.
For 11 years I had three incredible business partners, who helped lay a foundation for my development and contributed to making me the entrepreneur I am today. Joachim Karnath, Irene Raufenhauser and Judith Haupt... thank you! Even though I ended the business journey with you to start another business I do see the years with you as an incredible experience.

In 2017, I joined a business network called The Entrepreneurs' Organisation (EO) (www.eonetwork.org). I joined their Accelerator programme, which is all about scaling your business. This helped me look at entrepreneurship differently and showed me what I needed to focus on to grow and develop my business. I became more involved with EO and I was the Learning Chair for the Accelerator programme for a few years (a role I held even while writing this book). I was in an incredible position to have amazing entrepreneurs mentoring me. Yes, I'm going to name them as they all deserve a shout out for playing a direct or indirect role in the writing of this book. They are:

→ **Arlene Mulder** – Co-Founder of We Think Code – you introduced me to a network of entrepreneurs that have completely changed the course of my professional life. I can never thank you enough.

→ **Alon Sachs** – Co Founder of Mobelli Furniture+Living – yes, I listened. You said I should write a book and start doing talks. More importantly thank you for challenging me beyond my comfort zone every single time we chat.

→ **Arnie Shapiro** – Founder of Trematon – for the hours you spent with me when I bitched and moaned. Thank you for being supportive when I exited one business and started the next. You really do show me how to view things holistically.

→ **Richard Walton** – Founder of AVirtual and GVI – somehow you instilled a sense of loyalty in me and I never wanted to disappoint. I learn from you every day, particularly about work life integration and the importance of raising active kids in this beautiful city we live in

→ **Mike Scott** – Co Founder of NONA Digital – for opening my eyes about how to land messages in the digital world, steering me into building a profile and brand to be proud of.

→ **Danie Nel** – Founder of Nebula – for challenging my thinking on strategy at each EO learning day and for the valuable input you shared with regards to your own business processes.

acknowledgments

→ **Richard Mulholland** – Founder of Missing Link – thanks for the confidence boost, the keynote speaker development (which lead to me actually finishing this book) and just being a breath of fresh air.

I realised while writing this list how incredibly lucky I am. I haven't even mentioned my brothers and sister who impacted who I am and how I deal with things from a very young age. I could not have asked for better role models.

I'm sure I'm missing someone and I will never hear the end of it – bring it on and I'm sorry.

References

Berne, E. (1964) *Games People Play: The Psychology of Human*
Berne, E. (1977) *Intuition and ego states*
Covey, S. (1989) *The 7 Habits of Highly Effective People*
Green, H. and Howe, P. (2011) *The Trusted Advisor Fieldbook: A Comprehensive Toolkit for Leading with Trust*
Harnish, V. (2014) *Scaling Up: How a Few Companies Make It... and Why the Rest Don't*
Luft, L. (1969) *Of Human Interaction*
Manson, M. (2016) *The Subtle Art of Not Giving a F*ck*
Merrill D. and Reid, R. (1981) *Personal Styles & Effective Performance*
Switzler, A., Grenny J., and McMillan R. (2001) *Crucial Conversations: Tools for Talking When Stakes Are High*
Syed, M. (2015) *Black Box Thinking: Why Some People Never Learn from Their Mistakes – But Some Do*
Whitmore J. (2002) *Coaching For Performance: Growing People, Performance and Purpose*
Wickman, G. (2007) *Traction: Get A Grip On Your Business*

💬 About the author

HELÉNE SMUTS is an entrepreneur, avid reader and passionate traveller. As the founder of Credo Growth, she aims to bring out the best in leaders to help shape kick-ass teams.

Her career began in 2005 in Human Resources. In 2007, after she graduated cum laude in Industrial Psychology with an Honours degree from the University of South Africa, she started her first coaching practice called Credo Coaching. She merged her practice to co-found CONTRACT SA and spent 11 years developing high-performing teams across a variety of sectors. Her current client base at Credo Growth ranges from start-ups to blue-chip companies. Heléne has worked in an array of countries from her native South Africa to Europe, and North and South America.

When she isn't working on taking teams from mediocrity to *marvelocity*, Heléne enjoys spending quality time with her husband and twin girls, scuba diving, free diving in kelp forests, watching F1 Grand Prix races or trying to surf.

Resources

Did you love the book but want more guidelines, worksheets and videos? Become the leader everyone wants to follow with the online leadership course: Developing your own high performance team

Leadership course: http://bit.ly/hipteams

Action packed newsletter sign up page:

Newsletter: http://bit.ly/credonews

Scan for more info!

www.ingramcontent.com/pod-product-compliance
Lightning Source LLC
Chambersburg PA
CBHW070549090426
42735CB00013B/3122